A B
WITH ~~MANY POSSIBILITIES~~

With these daily readings, you can chart your course for romance, travel and adventure, good health, career opportunities and finances, and more as you gain insight into yourself and others. This guide provides forecasts based on lunar and planetary transits, and combines with the numerological readings specific to your sign and the day in question.

GENIE IN THE STARS ASTROLOGICAL GUIDE
Aries: Mar 21-Apr 19
Taurus: Apr 20 - May 20
Gemini: May 21-Jun 21
Cancer: Jun 22-Jul 22
Leo: Jul 23-Aug 22
Virgo: Aug 23-Sep 22
Libra: Sep 23-Oct 22
Scorpio: Oct 23-Nov 21
Sagittarius: Nov 22-Dec 21
Capricorn: Dec 22-Jan 19
Aquarius: Jan 20-Feb 18
Pisces: Feb 19-Mar 20

Panta Rei Press is an imprint of Crossroad Press Publishing

First edition

GENIE IN THE STARS

SAGITTARIUS

DAILY ASTROLOGICAL GUIDE FOR
2016

BY TRISH AND ROB MACGREGOR

PANTA REI

STAR STUFF

Since you picked up this book or ebook, then you're probably curious about or interested in astrology. So right off, you should know that one of the most valuable pieces of information you can have is your exact time of birth. As you read through this chapter, you'll understand why. But if you don't have the time, don't panic. There are ways around it.

How much do you know about the day you were born? What was the weather like that day? If you were born at night, had the moon already risen? Was it full or the shape of a Cheshire cat's grin? Was the delivery ward quiet or bustling with activity? Unless your mom or dad has a very good memory, you'll probably never know the full details. But there's one thing you can know for sure: on the day you were born, the sun was located in a particular zone of the zodiac, an imaginary 360-degree belt that circles the earth. The belt is divided into twelve 30-degree portions called signs.

If you were born between March 21 and April 19, then the sun was passing through the sign of Aries, so we say that your sun sign is Aries. Each of the twelve signs has distinct attributes and characteristics. Aries individuals, for example, are independent pioneers, fearless and passionate. Virgos, born between August 23 and September 22, are perfectionists with discriminating intellects and a genius for details. Geminis, born between May 21 and June 20, are networkers and communicators.

The twelve signs are categorized according to element and quality or modality. The first category reads like a basic science lesson—fire, earth, air and water—and describes the general physical characteristics of the signs.

- *Fire signs*—Aries, Leo, Sagittarius—are warm, dynamic individuals who are always passionate about what they do.
- *Earth signs*—Taurus, Virgo, Capricorn—are the builders of the zodiac, practical and efficient, grounded in everything they do.
- *Air signs*—Gemini, Libra, Aquarius—are people who live mostly in the world of ideas. They are terrific communicators.
- *Water signs*—Cancer, Scorpio, Pisces—live through their emotions, imaginations, and intuitions.

The second category describes how each sign operates in the physical world, how adaptable it is to circumstances.

- *Cardinal signs*—Aries, Cancer, Libra, Capricorn—are initiators. These people are active, impatient, restless. They're great at starting things, but unless a project or a relationship holds their attention, they lose interest and may not finish what they start.
- *Fixed signs*—Taurus, Leo, Scorpio, Aquarius—are deliberate, controlled. These individuals tend to move more slowly than cardinal signs, are often stubborn, and resist change. They seek roots, stability.
- *Mutable signs*—Gemini, Virgo, Sagittarius, Pisces— are adaptable. These people are flexible, changeable, communicative. They don't get locked into rigid patterns or belief systems.

TABLE 1 SUN SIGNS

Sign	Date	Element	Quality
Aries	Mar 21-Apr 19	Fire	Cardinal
Taurus	Apr 20 - May 20	Earth	Fixed
Gemini	May 21-Jun 21	Air	Mutable
Cancer	Jun 22-Jul 22	Water	Cardinal
Leo	Jul 23-Aug 22	Fire	Fixed
Virgo	Aug 23-Sep 22	Earth	Mutable
Libra	Sep 23-Oct 22	Air	Cardinal
Scorpio	Oct 23-Nov 21	Water	Fixed
Sagittarius	Nov 22-Dec 21	Fire	Mutable
Capricorn	Dec 22-Jan 19	Earth	Cardinal
Aquarius	Jan 20-Feb 18	Air	Fixed
Pisces	Feb 19-Mar 20	Water	Mutable

THE PLANETS

The planets in astrology are the players who make things happen. They're the characters in the story of your life. And this story always begins with the sun, the giver of life.

Your sun sign describes your self-expression, your primal energy, the essence of who you are. It's the archetypal pattern of your Self. When you know another person's sun sign, you already have a great deal of information about that person.

Let's say you're a Taurus who has just started dating a Gemini. How compatible are you? On the surface, it wouldn't seem that you have much in common. Taurus is a fixed earth sign; Gemini is a mutable air sign. Taurus is persistent, stubborn, practical, a cultivator as opposed to an initiator. Gemini is a chameleon, a communicator, social, with a mind as quick as lightning. Taurus is ruled by Venus, which governs the arts, money, beauty, love and romance, and Gemini is ruled by Mercury, which governs communication and travel. There doesn't seem to be much common ground. But before we write off this combination, let's look a little deeper.

Suppose the Taurus has Mercury in Gemini and suppose the Gemini has Venus in Taurus? This would mean that the Taurus and Gemini each have their rulers in the other person's sign. They probably communicate well and probably enjoy travel and books (Mercury) and would see eye to eye on romance, art, and music (Venus). They might get along so well, in fact, that they collaborate on creative projects.

Each of us is also influenced by the other nine planets (the sun and moon are treated like planets in astrology) and the signs they were transiting when you were born. Suppose your Taurus and Gemini children have the same moon sign? The moon rules our inner needs, emotions and intuition, and all that makes us feel secure within ourselves. Quite often, compatible moon signs can overcome even the most glaring differences in sun signs because the two people share similar emotions.

In the sections on monthly predictions, your sun sign always takes center stage and every prediction is based on the movement of the transiting planets in relation to your sun sign. Let's say you're a Sagittarius. Between October 18 and November 11 this year, Venus will be transiting your sign. What's this mean for you? Well, since Venus rules—among other things—romance, you can expect your love life to pick up significantly during these weeks. Other people will find you attractive, be more open to your ideas, and you'll radiate a certain charisma. Your creative endeavors will move full steam ahead.

Table 2 provides an overview of the planets and the signs that they rule. Keep in mind that the moon is the swiftest-moving planet, changing signs about every two and a half days, and that Pluto is the snail of the zodiac, taking as long as thirty years to transit a single sign. The other faster-moving planets transit a sign in weeks— Mercury, Venus, and Mars—and have an impact on our lives. But it's the slow pokes –Uranus, Neptune, and Pluto—that bring about the most profound influence and change. Jupiter and Saturn fall between the others in terms of speed.

In the section on predictions, the most frequent references are to the transits of the Mercury, Venus, and Mars. In the daily predictions for each sign, the predictions are based primarily on the transiting moon.

Now glance through table 2. When a sign is in parenthesis, it means the planet co-rules that sign. This assignation dates back to when we thought there were only seven planets in the solar system. But since there were still twelve signs, some of the planets had to do double duty!

TABLE 2—THE PLANETS

Planet	Rules	Attributes of Planet
Sun	Leo	Self-expression, primal energy, creative ability, ego, individuality
Moon	Cancer	Emotions, intuition, mother or wife, security
Mercury	Gemini (Virgo)	Intellect, mental acuity, communication, logic, reasoning, travel, contracts
Venus	Taurus (Libra)	Love, romance, beauty, artistic instincts, the arts, music, material and financial resources
Mars	Aries (Scorpio)	Physical and sexual energy, aggression, drive
Jupiter	Sagittarius (Pisces)	Luck, expansion, success, prosperity, growth, creativity, spiritual interest higher education, law
Saturn	Capricorn (Aquarius)	Laws of physical universe, discipline, structure, responsibility, karma, authority
Uranus	Aquarius	Individuality, genius, eccentricity, originality, revolution
Neptune	Pisces	Visionary self, illusions, what's hidden, psychic ability, spiritual insights, dreams
Pluto	Scorpio	The darker side, death, sex, regeneration, rebirth, profound and permanent change, transformation

HOUSES & RISING SIGNS

In the instant you drew your first breath, one of the signs of the zodiac was just passing over the eastern horizon. Astrologers refer to this as the rising sign or ascendant. It's what makes your horoscope unique. Think of your ascendant as the front door of your horoscope, the place where you enter into this life and begin your journey.

Your ascendant is based on the exact moment of your birth and the other signs follow counterclockwise. If you have Taurus rising, for example, that is the cusp of your first house. The cusp of the second would be Gemini, of the third Cancer, and so on around the horoscope circle in a counterclockwise direction. Each house governs a particular area of life, which is outlined below.

The best way to find out your rising sign is to have your horoscope drawn up by an astrologer. There are also sites in the Internet that provide free charts. One of the best is here: http://alabe.com/freechart.

In a horoscope, the ascendant (cusp of the first house), IC (cusp of the fourth house), Descendent (cusp of the seventh house) and MC (cusp of the tenth house) are considered to be the most critical angles. Any planets that fall close to these angles are extremely important in the overall astrological picture of who you are. By the same token, planets that fall in the first, fourth, seventh, and tenth houses are also considered to be important.

Now here's a rundown on what the houses mean.

ASCENDANT OR RISING: THE FIRST OF FOUR IMPORTANT CRITICAL ANGLES IN A HOROSCOPE

- How other people see you
- How you present yourself to the world
- Your physical appearance

1ST HOUSE. PERSONALITY

- Early childhood
- Your ego
- Your body type and how you feel about your body
- General physical health
- Defense mechanisms
- Your creative thrust

2ND HOUSE. PERSONAL VALUES

- How you earn and spend your money
- Your personal values
- Your material resources and assets
- Your attitudes toward money
- Your possessions and your attitude toward those possessions
- Your self-worth
- Your attitudes toward creativity

3RD HOUSE. COMMUNICATION & LEARNING

- Personal expression
- Intellect and mental attitudes & perceptions
- Siblings, neighbors, and relatives
- How you learn
- School until college
- Reading, writing, teaching
- Short trips (the grocery store versus Europe in 7 days)
- Earth-bound transportation
- Creativity as a communication device

IC OR 4TH HOUSE CUSP
THE SECOND CRITICAL ANGLE IN A HOROSCOPE

- Sign on IC describes the qualities and traits of your home and family life during early childhood
- Describes roots of your creative abilities and talents

4TH HOUSE, YOUR ROOTS

- Personal environment
- Your home
- Your attitudes toward family
- Early childhood conditioning
- Real estate
- The conditions at the end of your life
- Early childhood support of your creativity
- Your nurturing parent

Some astrologers say this house belongs to Mom or her equivalent in your life, others say it belongs to Dad or his equivalent. It makes sense to me that it's Mom because the fourth house is ruled by the Moon, which rules mothers. But in this day and age, when parental roles are in flux, the only hard and fast rule is that the fourth belongs to the parent who nurtures you most of the time.

5TH HOUSE, CHILDREN AND CREATIVITY

- Kids, your first-born in particular
- Love affairs
- What you enjoy
- Gambling and speculation
- Creative ability
- Pets

Traditionally, pets belong in the sixth house. But that definition stems from the days when 'pets' were chattel. These days, they are animal companions who bring us pleasure.

6TH HOUSE, WORK & RESPONSIBILITY

- Day to day working conditions and environment
- Competence and skills
- Your experience of employees and employers
- Duty—to work, to employees
- Health
- Daily work approach to creativity
-

DESCENDANT 7TH HOUSE CUSP: THE THIRD CRITICAL ANGLE IN A HOROSCOPE

- The sign on the house cusp describes the qualities sought in intimate or business relationships
- Describes qualities of creative partnerships

7TH HOUSE, PARTNERSHIPS AND MARRIAGE

- Marriage
- Marriage partner
- Significant others
- Business partnerships
- Close friends
- Open enemies
- Contracts

8TH HOUSE TRANSFORMATION

- Sexuality as transformation
- Secrets
- Death, taxes, inheritances
- Resources shared with others
- Your partner's finances
- The occult (read: astrology, reincarnation, UFOs, everything weird and strange)
- Your hidden talents
- Psychology
- Life-threatening illnesses
- Your creative depths

9TH HOUSE. WORLDVIEW

- Philosophy and religion
- The law, courts, judicial system
- Publishing
- Foreign travels and cultures
- College, graduate school
- Spiritual beliefs and worldview

MC OR CUSP OF 10TH HOUSE: THE FOURTH CRITICAL ANGLE IN A HOROSCOPE

- Sign on cusp of MC describes qualities you seek in a profession
- Your public image
- Your creative and professional achievements

10TH HOUSE. PROFESSION & CAREER

- Your profession/career as opposed to a job that merely pays the bills (sixth house)
- Your status and position in the world
- The authoritarian parent and authority in general
- People who hold power over you
- Your public life
- Your career/profession

11TH HOUSE. IDEALS & DREAMS

- Peer groups
- Social circles (your writers' group, your mother's bridge club)
- Your dreams and aspirations
- How you can realize your creative dreams

12ᵗʜ HOUSE, PERSONAL UNCONSCIOUS

- Power you have disowned that must be reclaimed
- Institutions—hospitals, prisons, nursing homes, what is hidden
- What you must confront this time around, your karma, issues brought in from other lives
- Psychic gifts and abilities
- Healing talents
- What you give unconditionally

In the section on predictions, you'll find references to transiting planets moving into certain houses. These houses are actually solar houses that are created by putting your sun sign on the ascendant. This technique is how most predictions are made for the general public rather than for specific individuals.

LUNATIONS

Every year, there are twelve new moons and twelve full moons, with some years having thirteen moons. In 2016, there's an extra new moon. New moons are typically when we should begin new projects, set new goals, seek new opportunities. They're times for beginnings.

Two weeks after each new moon, there's a full moon. This is the time of harvest, fruition, when we reap what we've sown.

Whenever a new moon falls in your sign, take time to brainstorm what you would like to achieve during weeks and months until the full moon falls in your sign. These goals can be in any area of your life. Or, you can simply take the time on each new moon to set up goals and strategies for what you would like to achieve or manifest during the next two weeks—until the full moon—or until the next new moon.

Here's a list of all the new moons and full moons during 2016. The asterisk beside any new moon entry indicates a solar eclipse; the asterisk next to a full moon entry indicates a lunar eclipse.

New Moons	Full Moons
January 9 Capricorn	January 23 Leo
February 8 Aquarius	February 22 Virgo
March 8 Pisces*	March 23 Libra*
April 7 Aries	April 21 Scorpio
May 6 Taurus	May 21 Sagittarius
June 4 Gemini	June 20 Sagittarius
July 4 Cancer	July 19 Capricorn
August 2 Leo	August 18 Aquarius*
September 1 Virgo*	September 16 Pisces*
September 30 Libra	October 15 Aries
October 30 Scorpio	November 14 Taurus
November 29 Sagittarius	December 13 Gemini
December 28 Capricorn	

In 2016, there are five eclipses—two solar and three lunar. But most years feature two lunar and two solar eclipses, separated from each other by about two weeks. Lunar eclipses tend to deal with emotional issues, our internal world, and often bring an emotional issue to the surface related to the sign and house in which the eclipse falls. Solar eclipses deal with events and often enable us to see something that has eluded us. They also symbolize beginnings and endings.

Look to the entries for that month for more information. I also recommend Celeste Teal's excellent book, *Eclipses*.

MERCURY RETROGRADE

Every year, Mercury—the planet that symbolizes communication and travel—turns retrograde three times. During these periods, your travel plans often go awry, you face unexpected delays, communication breaks down, computers go berserk, cars or appliances develop problems. You get the idea. Things in our daily lives don't work as smoothly as we would like. These retrogrades are noted in the daily predictions.

CONTACT US

Please contact us with any questions you have www.genieinthesky.com or through our other websites or blog:

www.robmacgregor.buzz
www.trishjmacgregor.com
www.synchrosecrets.com
blog.synchrosecrets.com

BY THE NUMBERS

Even though this is an astrology book, we combine numerology to some of the daily predictions to provide a deeper look at the day's possibilities. So let's take a closer look at how the numbers come into play.

If you're familiar with numerology, you probably know your life path number, which is derived from your birth date. That number represents who you were at birth and the traits that you'll carry throughout your life. You can find numerous web sites that provide details on what the numbers mean regarding your life path.

But in the daily predictions, what does it mean when it's a number 9 day, and how did it get to be that number? In the dailies, you'll usually find these numbers on the days when the moon is transiting from one sign to another. The system is simple: add the numbers related to the astrological sign (1 for Aries, 2 for Taurus, etc.), the year, the month, and the day.

For example, to find what number January 15, 2016 is for a Libra, you would start with 7, the number for Libra, the seventh sign of the zodiac, add 9, the number you get when you add 2016 together, plus 1 for January, and 6 (1+5) for the day. That would be 7+9+1+6 (sign+year+month+date) = 23=5 (2+3). So January 15, 2016 is a 5 day for a Libra. It would be a 6 day for a Scorpio, the sign following Libra.

So on that day, Libra might be advised: Change and variety are highlighted now. Think freedom, think outside the box. No restrictions. Your creativity, personal grace and magnetism are highlighted.

Here's a summary of the meanings of the numbers, which are included with more detail in the daily predictions. Keep in mind that the dailies might also take into account the moon sign for the day, the house the moon is in, and the sun sign.

1. Taking the lead, getting a fresh start, a new beginning.
2. Cooperation, partnership, a new relationship, sensitivity.
3. Harmony, beauty, pleasures of life, warm and receptive.
4. Getting organized, hard work, being methodical, rebuilding, fulfilling your obligations.
5. Freedom of thought and action, change, variety, thinking outside the box.
6. A service day, being diplomatic, generous, tolerant, sympathetic.
7. Mystery, secrets, investigations, research, detecting deception, exploration of the unknown, of the spiritual realms.
8. Your power day, financial success, unexpected money, a windfall
9. Finishing a project, looking beyond the immediate, setting your goals, reflection, expansion.

Simple, right?

Once you become accustomed to what the numbers mean for a particular day, you can adjust your attitude, thoughts, and actions accordingly. After all, how your day, week, or month unfolds depends more on your attitude toward yourself and your world than it does on any number or astrology sign.

If you practice waking up each morning in a spirit of adventure and gratitude, then pretty soon it becomes second nature, and your life shifts accordingly. Sound like magical thinking? Indeed it is, and when you discover your innate power to change your life for the better, you recognize the world is a magical place.

OVERVIEW OF SAGITTARIUS PERSONALITY

Oh, baby, let the good times roll! And for Sadge, those good times mean music, deep talk, exotic travel, esoteric ideas, a continual quest to understand the universe in which you live. At heart, you're an explorer and how the expression of that eagerness depends entirely on your free will. In one form or another, the search for a higher truth is what you're about.

Even though you may go for years without being able to identify the inner itch that propels you from one experience to another, at some point you're able to pinpoint the source of it. That moment of illumination may be triggered by an external event, a relationship, travel, a health issue, or some inner experience that literally transforms you.

You're often blunt when dealing with others, particularly when the other guy just doesn't get what seems so obvious to you. Patience and nuance aren't your strong points. The exception to this occurs when you're pursuing something about which you feel passionate, then you have the patience of Mother Theresa and are as detail-oriented as a Virgo.

Like your fire cousin, Aries, your thing is action. You would rather do than think about doing. As a mutable sign, you're emotionally adaptable. You have opinions about virtually everything and aren't the least bit hesitant in expressing these opinions. This becomes a problem if you're dogmatic or bombastic about what you believe and try to convert others to your way of thinking. You're great at grasping the *big picture*. The challenge is to see the trees as clearly as you do the forest and to relate it to your daily life. With practice, your intuition can provide the essential details of that larger picture.

DAILY PREDICTIONS—2016

January

- *Friday, January 1 (Moon into Libra, 1:42 am)*
  Mercury moves into your third house today, indicating that you're versatile and adaptable now and you communicate well, especially with neighbors and relatives. You could be talking about a matter from the past.

- *Saturday, January 2 (Moon in Libra)*
  The moon is in your eleventh house today. Friends play an important role in your day, especially Libra and Aquarius, and you take the initiative to get together with them. You find strength in numbers, and meaning through friends and groups. Social consciousness plays a role.

- *Sunday, January 3 (Moon into Scorpio, 2:37 pm)*
  Mars moves into your twelfth house today and stays there until March 5. That means you have lots of energy now while you're working behind the scenes in secret. Your desires and actions are influenced by your subconscious mind and matters from the past. You have a strong sense of mission now, but you're keeping it to yourself. Unconscious anger needs to be brought to the surface and resolved.

- *Monday, January 4 (Moon in Scorpio)*
  Think carefully before you act today. There's a tendency now to undo all the positive actions you've taken. Avoid any self-destructive tendencies. Be aware of hidden enemies. It's a good day to work behind the scenes. Matters affecting the past, even your childhood play a role.

- *Tuesday, January 5 (Moon in Scorpio)*
  Mercury goes retrograde today in your third house and stays that way until January 25. There could be some miscommunication and misunderstanding with siblings, relatives or neighbors. A matter from the past could cause some confusion now. Expect delays and glitches as you go about your everyday world. Don't worry, it won't last.

- *Wednesday, January 6 (Moon into Sagittarius, 1:57 am)*
  It's a number 7 day, your mystery day. Secrets, intrigue, confidential information play a role today. You might feel best working on your own. You investigate, analyze or simply observe what's going on now. You quickly come to a conclusion and wonder why others don't see what you see. It's best to hold off on making any final decisions for a couple of days.

- *Thursday, January 7 (Moon in Sagittarius)*
  Jupiter goes retrograde in your tenth house today, where it remains until May 9. That means work activity slows down. Whatever you were doing in your career that was expanding or expansiveness in nature, shrinks back now for a few months. It's a good time to re-work and improve your product. Your associates will understand the need to make some changes before you move ahead.

- *Friday, January 8 (Moon into Capricorn, 10:07 am)*
  It's a number 9 day. That means it's all about beginnings and endings. Finish what you started. Visualize the future; set your goals, then make them so. Look beyond the immediate. Find a new approach, a new perspective. Spiritual values play a role. You could be feeling restless today and sending text messages or e-mails to friends and associates to pass the time.

- *Saturday, January 9 (Moon in Capricorn)*
  There's a new moon in your second house today. That means new opportunities come your way that could provide new sources of income. You get a new beginning, and new insight into your values. You identify emotionally with your possessions or whatever you value.

- *Sunday, January 10 (Moon into Aquarius, 3:23 pm)*
  It's a number 2 day. Don't make waves. Don't rush or show resentment. Let things develop. You're diplomatic and capable of fixing whatever has gone wrong. Use your intuition when dealing with others. You're ambitious in pursuing a partnership. Cooperation is highlighted.

- *Monday, January 11 (Moon in Aquarius)*
  The moon is in your third house today. You're dealing with neighbors, friends and family members. You could be embarking on a short trip that might involve siblings or relatives. Take what you know and share it with others. You communicate well today, but stay in conscious control of your emotions, especially in dealing with people you encounter in your everyday life. Matters from the past could come up.

- *Tuesday, January 12 (Moon into Pisces, 6:54 pm)*
  It's a number 4 day. That means your organizational skills are called upon, Sadge. Persevere to get things done today. Hard work is called for. Be methodical and thorough. Tear down the old in order to rebuild. You're developing a creative base for the future.

- *Wednesday, January 13 (Moon in Pisces)*
  With the moon in your fourth house, it's a good day spruce up your home. You also could be dealing with parents now. You feel a close tie to your roots. Focus on changing a bad habit today.

- *Thursday, January 14 (Moon into Aries, 9:49 pm)*
  It's a number 6 day, a service day. Be understanding and avoid confrontations. Diplomacy wins the way. Focus on making people happy, but avoid scattering your energies.

- *Friday, January 15 (Moon in Aries)*
  The moon is in your fifth house today. Your love life takes off now. You can expand a relationship now. There's also an idealistic turn to whatever you do for pleasure. It's a great time for a creative project, especially fiction writing. You could be

somewhat possessive of loved ones and children today. It's a good day to get a pet!

- *Saturday, January 16 (Moon in Aries)*
  You're extremely persuasive now, especially if you're passionate about what you're doing or selling or trying to convey. You imprint your own style. It's a good day to start something new. However, avoid reckless actions that could cause you grief. Emotions could be volatile. You're passionate, but impatient.

- *Sunday, January 17 (Moon into Taurus, 00:49 am)*
  It's a number 9 day. Visualize the future; set your goals, then make them so. Look beyond the immediate. Look for a new approach, a new perspective. Remain optimistic, Aries. The old cycle is ending, a new one about to begin. Visualize the future; set your goals, then make them so.

- *Monday, January 18 (Moon in Taurus)*
  The moon is in your sixth house today. It's a service day and you're at your best helping others now. You're the one others go to for guidance. Make yourself available, but don't deny your own needs. Keep your resolutions about exercise and watch your diet.

- *Tuesday, January 19 (Moon into Gemini, 4:14 am)*
  It's a number 2 day. The spotlight shines on cooperative efforts. If you're married, your marriage takes on more significance and brings in more structure to your life. If you're not married, there could be some soul-searching related to a relationship, or a new relationship developing. Help comes through friends today.

- *Wednesday, January 20 (Moon in Gemini)*
  With the moon in your seventh house today, the focus turns to partnerships, both personal and professional. Focus on ways to expand, but be careful how you deal with disagreements. Any conflict will be more emotional than usual now. It's difficult to remain detached and objective.

- *Thursday, January 21 (Moon into Cancer, 8:29 am)*
It's a number 4 day, and a good one to spend time on getting organized. Be practical with your money. Take care of your obligations and control your impulses to wander off, Sadge. Persevere to get things done. You're building a foundation for the future. Hard work is called for now.

- *Friday, January 22 (Moon in Cancer)*
The moon is in your eighth house today. It's a good time to deal with any matters related to taxes, insurance or investments. Be aware that emotions can get intense now, especially when dealing with shared resources. You could take an interest in a metaphysical topic now, such as life after death or past lives.

- *Saturday, January 23 (Moon into Leo, 2:22 pm)*
There's a full moon in Leo, your ninth house, today. You're in a good position to break away from the usual routine and possibly pursue long-distance travel. You reap what you've sown, and you benefit from your association with a foreign-born person or a foreign country. Look to the big picture.

- *Sunday, January 24 (Moon in Leo)*
The moon is again in your ninth house, your native home, Sadge. You see the big picture, but you sometimes have trouble seeing the trees because you're so enamored by the forest. A foreign country or person of foreign birth could play a role. Philosophy, religion, or mythology plays a role in your day.

- *Monday, January 25 (Moon into Virgo, 10:47 pm)*
Mercury goes direct in your second house today. Any confusion, miscommunication and delays related to money matters recedes into the past. Things move more smoothly now. You're clear on your values, and get your message across. Everything works better now, including computers and other electronic equipment.

- *Tuesday, January 26 (Moon in Virgo)*
Professional concerns are the focus of the day. Business dealings are highlighted. It's a great day for sales. You're more emotional

and warm toward co-workers, but don't blur boundary between personal and professional lives.

- *Wednesday, January 27 (Moon in Virgo)*
  Take care of details now, especially related to your health. Remember to exercise and watch your diet. Stop worrying and fretting. Stick close to home, if possible, focus on tidying up the house. You may exhibit some perfectionist tendencies now.

- *Thursday, January 28 (Moon into Libra, 10 am)*
  Partnerships are highlighted. Use your intuition to get a sense of your day and focus on relationships. Be kind and understanding. The spotlight is on cooperation. Emotions and your sensitivity play a role.

- *Friday, January 29 (Moon in Libra)*
  It's a number 2 day. The spotlight shines on cooperative efforts. If you're married, your marriage takes on more significance and brings in more structure to your life. If you're not married, there could be some soul-searching related to a relationship, or a new relationship developing. Help comes through friends today.

- *Saturday, January 30 (Moon into Scorpio, 10:51 pm)*
  Your organizational skills are highlighted today. Control your impulses. Take care of your obligations. You're building foundations for an outlet for your creativity, Leo. Emphasize quality. Be methodical and thorough.

- *Sunday, January 31 (Moon in Scorpio)*
  The moon is in your twelfth house today. Best to work behind the scenes today and avoid any conflicts and confrontations, especially with women. Keep your feelings secret. Unconscious attitudes can be difficult.

FEBRUARY

- *Monday, February 1 (Moon in Scorpio)*
  With the moon in your twelfth house today, you tend to withdraw from public view. Unconscious attitudes can be difficult now. So can relations with women. Keep your feelings secret. Work behind the scenes, and follow your intuition.

- *Tuesday, February 2 (Moon into Sagittarius, 10:50 am)*
  It's a number 4 day. That means your organizational skills are called upon now. You're building foundations for the future, developing outlets for your creativity. Stay focused and emphasize quality in whatever you're doing.

- *Wednesday, February 3 (Moon in Sagittarius)*
  The moon is in your first house today. Your self-awareness or appearance is important now. You're dealing with the person you are becoming, Sadge. You have opinions about virtually everything and aren't the least bit hesitant in expressing them. You're emotionally adaptable. You may feel moody, withdrawn one moment, happy the next, then sad. It's all about your emotional self. Your feelings and thoughts are aligned.

- *Thursday, February 4 (Moon into Capricorn, 7:44 pm)*
  It's a number 6 day. That means a domestic shift of priorities might be needed now, Sagittarius. Be understanding and avoid confrontations. Diplomacy wins the way. Focus on making people happy, but avoid scattering your energies.

- *Friday, February 5 (Moon in Capricorn)*
  The moon is in your second house today. Money issues matters take priority now. You seek both financial and domestic security now. You identify emotionally with your possessions or whatever you value. Look at your priorities in handling your income. Take care of payments and collect what's owed to you.

- *Saturday, February 6 (Moon in Capricorn)*
  Your ambition and drive to succeed are highlighted. Authority figures or elderly people play a role. Your responsibilities increase. You may feel stressed and overworked, but don't ignore your exercise routine. Maintain emotional balance. Be conservative, don't speculate or take any unnecessary risks.

- *Sunday, February 7 (Moon into Aquarius, 1 am)*
  It's a number 9 day. Visualize for the future, and strive for universal appeal. Set your goals, then make them so. You're up to the challenge. Complete a project and get ready for something new coming up.

- *Monday, February 8 (Moon in Aquarius)*
  With the new moon in your third house today, Sadge, an opportunity related to something from the past comes your way. Siblings, relatives or neighbors could play a role. Take what you know and share it with others. Pay attention to how people respond.

- *Tuesday, February 9 (Moon into Pisces, 3:32 am)*
  It's a number 2 day. Partnerships play an important role in your day. Cooperation is highlighted. Use your intuition to get a sense of your day. Try not to rock the boat.

- *Wednesday, February 10 (Moon in Pisces)*
  The moon is in your fourth house today. You're dealing with your home life and the foundations of who you are. Spend time with family and loved ones. Take the day off, if possible, or work at home. It's a good day to handle repairs on your home. Spend some time in meditation.

- *Thursday, February 11 (Moon into Aries, 4:56 am)*
  It's a number 4 day. Control any impulses to wander off task. Stay focused, fulfill your obligations. You're building a creative base. It's a day of hard work that will make next month go easier. Romance goes onto the back burner today.

- *Friday, February 12 (Moon in Aries)*
  The moon is in your fifth house today. It's a great day for pursuing romance. There's greater emotional depth in whatever you seek. Be yourself, be emotionally honest. You're creative now and have the ability to tap deeply into the collective unconscious. Children and pets could play a role.

- *Saturday, February 13 (Moon into Taurus, 6:37 am)*
  Mercury moves into your third house today. Your mind is busy jumping from one subject to another. You see both side of a dispute, and you also see your side. You communicate well and others just try to keep up with you. You're at center stage, Sadge.

- *Sunday, February 14 (Moon in Taurus)*
  The moon is in your sixth house today. It's another service day. Others recognize your energy and call on you for help. Offer assistance, but don't deny your own needs. Visit someone who is ill, do a good deed. But pay attention to any health matters now. Exercise and watch your diet.

- *Monday, February 15 (Moon into Gemini, 9:36 am)*
  It's a number 8 day, your lucky money day. You attract financial success. Unexpected money arrives. Expect a windfall. You can go far with your plans and achieve financial success. You have a chance to expand, to gain recognition, fame and power.

- *Tuesday, February 16 (Moon in Gemini)*
  Venus moves into your third house today. Your positive relationship with siblings and relatives works to your benefit. You mental abilities are strong now and you have an emotional need to reinvigorate your studies, especially regarding matters of the past. It's a good time for writing and getting your work published.

- *Wednesday, February 17 (Moon into Cancer, 2:25 pm)*
  It's a number 1 day. That means you're at the top of your cycle again, Sadge. You get a fresh start now. Be independent and avoid negative people. It's a great time for starting something new. Surround yourself with creative and adventurous one. Trust your hunches and don't be afraid to turn in a new direction.

- *Thursday, February 18 (Moon in Cancer)*
  The moon is in your eighth house today. Security matters dominate your thoughts now and can affect your feelings about your belongings, as well as things that you share with others, such as a spouse. If you are planning on making a major purchase, make sure that you and your partner are in agreement. Otherwise, you could encounter intense emotional resistance. You could be dealing with taxes or insurance today.

- *Friday, February 19 (Moon into Leo, 9:18 pm)*
  It's a number 3 day. Take time to relax, enjoy yourself, recharge your batteries. You can influence people now with your upbeat attitude. Your charm and wit are appreciated. Foster generosity. In romance, you're an ardent lover and loyal.

- *Saturday, February 20 (Moon in Leo)*
  The moon is in your ninth house today. You yearn for new experiences now. You have an interest in new ideas and you can create positive change through them. You seek a change from the routine, a break from the status quo. It's a good day to plan a long trip.

- *Sunday, February 21 (Moon in Leo)*
  Theatrics and drama are highlighted today, perhaps involving children. You're at center stage. You're ready to flaunt and celebrate. Be wild, imaginative, be the person you always imagined you might be. Play with different personas. Be yourself. Be emotionally honest. In love, there's greater emotional depth to a relationship now. Embrace what you love, who you love.

- *Monday, February 22 (Moon into Virgo, 6:25 am)*
  There's also a full moon in your tenth house today. You reap what you've sown. It's a time of completion. You finish one thing and get ready for something new. At the same time, you gain insight into matters related to your career. You get a new perspective, a better understanding, possibly about your boss or fellow workers.

- *Tuesday, February 23 (Moon in Virgo)*
  The moon remains in your tenth house of career. Professional concerns are the focus of the day. Business dealings are highlighted. An advancement, a raise, or bonus is coming your way. Go for it, Sadge. You gain a boost of prestige.

- *Wednesday, February 24 (Moon into Libra, 5:42 pm)*
  It's another number 8 day, a power day, and another chance for a big windfall. It's a good day to play the lotto. Unexpected money arrives. You can pull a power play now, but be careful not to hurt others.

- *Thursday, February 25 (Moon in Libra)*
  The moon is in your eleventh house today. Friends play an important role in your day, especially Aries and Leo. You work well with a group and find strength in numbers, especially if you're with a group of like-minded people working for the common good.

- *Friday, February 26 (Moon in Libra)*
  Romance is highlighted. Relationships issues figure prominently in your day. Museums, art, music, creativity all figure in. It's a day for feeding your creative juices. Your personal grace and magnetism, and physical attraction play a role.

- *Saturday, February 27 (Moon into Scorpio, 6:27 am)*
  It's a number 2 day. Use your intuition to get a sense of your day. Be kind and understanding. Cooperation, especially with partners, is highlighted. Don't make waves. Don't rush or show resentment. Let things develop. Marriage plays a key role.

- *Sunday, February 28 (Moon in Scorpio)*
  The moon is in your twelfth house today. It's a great day for a mystical or spiritual discipline. Your intuition is heightened. However, unconscious attitudes can be difficult now. So can relations with women. It's a good time for therapy, and working behind the scenes.

- *Monday, February 29 (Moon in Scorpio)*
  Secrets, intrigue, confidential information play a role. You work best on your own today. Knowledge is essential to success. Gather information, but don't make any absolute decisions until tomorrow. Go with the flow.

MARCH

- **Tuesday, March 1 (Moon into Sagittarius)**
  You're a dreamer and a thinker, Sadge. Look to the big picture. Higher education and the higher mind are highlighted. You may feel a need to get away now, a break from the usual routine. You yearn for a new experience. Tomorrow could be the day.

- **Wednesday, March 2 (Moon in Sagittarius)**
  With the moon is on your ascendant today the way you see yourself now is the way others see you. You're feeling recharged and ready to go. You're physically vital, and relations with the opposite sex go well. Your appearance and personality shines.

- **Thursday, March 3 (Moon into Capricorn, 5:02 am)**
  It's a number 6 day. Service to others is the theme of the day. You offer advice and support. Be sympathetic and kind, generous and tolerant. Focus on making people happy. However, avoid scattering your energies.

- **Friday, March 4 (Moon in Capricorn)**
  The moon is in your second house today. Expect emotional experiences related to money. You identify emotionally with your possessions or whatever you value. Look at your priorities in handling your income. Put off making any major purchases now.

- **Saturday, March 5 (Moon into Aquarius, 11:23 am)**
  Mars moves into your third house today. You're witty and aggressive in presenting your ideas. It's easy for you to get

impatient with those who aren't up to your speed. That's especially true of family members, relatives, and neighbors. Try not to rush and do your best to avoid arguments. With Mercury moving into your fifth house, you communicate well about a creative project.

- *Sunday, March 6 (Moon in Aquarius)*
  The moon is in your third house today. Your communications with others are subjective. Take what you know and share it with others, but control your emotions. That's especially true when dealing with siblings and relatives, or neighbors. Your thinking is unduly influenced by things of the past.

- *Monday, March 7 (Moon into Pisces, 2:10 pm)*
  It's a number 1 day and you're at the top of your cycle. Get out and meet new people, have new experiences, do something you've never done before. You're inspired to turn your career in a new direction. Don't fear change. In romance, a flirtation turns more serious.

- *Tuesday, March 8 (Moon in Pisces)*
  There's a new moon in your fourth house today. New opportunities come your way related to home. If you're selling or buying a home, you could get a contract now. It's also a good day to work on a home repair project or work at home. Don't be surprised if the opportunity arises from a call from family members who live far away.

- *Wednesday, March 9 (Moon into Aries, 2:41)*
  It's a number 3 day. You are relaxed, but attentive today. Your imagination is keen now. You're curious and inventive. You communicate well today. Enjoy the harmony, beauty and pleasures of life. Beautify your home. Remain flexible. Your attitude determines everything today.

- *Thursday, March 10 (Moon in Aries)*
  The moon is in your fifth house today. Your love life takes off now. You can expand a relationship now. There's also an

idealistic turn to whatever you do for pleasure. It's a great time for a creative project, especially fiction writing. You could be somewhat possessive of loved ones and children today. It's a good day to get a pet!

- *Friday, March 11 (Moon into Taurus, 2:45 pm)*
It's a number 5 day. That means it's a good day to promote new ideas. You're versatile, changeable. Be careful not to spread out and diversify too much. Freedom of thought and action are key. A change of scenery would work to your advantage.

- *Saturday, March 12 (Moon in Taurus)*
Venus moves into your fourth house today. It's a good day for your love life. Stay home and cuddle with your sweetheart. Beautify your home, or work on an artistic or creative project in your home.

- *Sunday, March 13 (Moon into Gemini, 5:04 pm)*
It's a number 7 day. Secrets, intrigue, confidential information play a role. Investigate activities taking place behind closed doors. You work best on your own today. Keep your own counsel. Knowledge is essential to success. Gather information, but don't make any absolute decisions until tomorrow. Daylight saving time begins.

- *Monday, March 14 (Moon in Gemini)*
The moon is in your seventh house today. Partnerships are highlighted. Focus on personal relationships. Loved ones play a major role. Be aware that any conflicts, especially with women, will be more emotional than usual. You could have a difficult time remaining detached and objective.

- *Tuesday, March 15 (Moon into Cancer, 8:57 pm)*
It's a number 9 day. Complete a project now. Clear up odds and ends. Take an inventory on where things are going in your life. Visualize the future; set your goals, then make them so. Accept what comes your way now. It's all part of a cycle.

- *Wednesday, March 16 (Moon in Cancer)*
  The moon is in your eighth house today. Your experience might turn more intense now, especially if you're dealing with shared possessions. You could attract powerful people to you. An interest in metaphysics plays a role. Sex, death, and rebirth could be current themes. You explore life's mysteries, including what happens at the end of life.

- *Thursday, March 17 (Moon in Cancer)*
  You're feeling intuitive and nurturing today. You also could feel moody and overly sensitive. Best to keep your thoughts to yourself. Your home life takes on new importance. It's a good day to work at home.

- *Friday, March 18 (Moon into Leo, 3:55 am)*
  It's a number 3 day. Take time to relax, enjoy yourself, recharge your batteries. You can influence people now with your upbeat attitude. Your charm and wit are appreciated. Foster generosity. In romance, you're an ardent lover and loyal.

- *Saturday, March 19 (Moon in Leo)*
  With the moon in your ninth house, you need to get away from your usual routine today. You're feeling restless, Sadge. It's a good day to plan that long trip or sign up for a seminar or workshop that interests you. A publishing project goes well.

- *Sunday, March 20 (Moon into Virgo, 1:40 pm)*
  It's a number 5 day. Promote new ideas, follow your curiosity. Approach the day with an unconventional mindset. Release old structures, get a new point of view. Think freedom, no restrictions. Variety is the spice of life.

- *Monday, March 21 (Moon in Virgo)*
  Mercury moves into your fifth house today. The creative and romantic energy of the last few days continues. You can express yourself, Sadge, in a dramatic and forceful manner, this month to make your point. You're mentally stimulated, and you might be analyzing a romance this month.

- *Tuesday, March 22 (Moon in Virgo)*
  With the moon in your tenth house today, professional concerns take priority now. Business is highlighted. You're feeling warm toward fellow workers, but make sure you don't let your professional and personal lives mix now.

- *Wednesday, March 23 (Moon into Libra, 1:24 am)*
  There's a lunar eclipse in your tenth house today. You gain insight into a matter dealing with your career. Co-workers could play a role. If you feel that you need to take control of the situation, make sure others are informed of what you're doing. Whatever the issue that comes up, it's a serious one.

- *Thursday, March 24 (Moon in Libra)*
  The moon is in your eleventh house today. Friends play an important role in your day. You benefit as a result of social contacts. You're warm and receptive to what others say, especially those involved in a group. Your charm and wit are appreciated. You tend to surround yourself now with creative people.

- *Friday, March 25, (Moon into Scorpio, 2:10 pm.)*
  Saturn turns retrograde in your first house today and stays that way until August 13. That means you could encounter emotional constraints in your personal life. Nothing moves very smoothly. It's a good time to review your goals to make sure they are still relevant to the person you are becoming. You might need to refocus your energy on a home improvement project and keep any disruptive thoughts to yourself during this time.

- *Saturday, March 26 (Moon in Scorpio)*
  The moon is in your twelfth house today. You might feel a need to withdraw and work on your own. Caution is the key word. Think carefully before you act. There's a tendency to undo all the positive actions you've taken. Avoid any self-destructive tendencies. Be aware of hidden enemies.

- *Sunday, March 27 (Moon in Scorpio)*
  With the moon remaining in Scorpio, intense, emotional experiences could play out today. You're passionate, Sadge, your sexuality is heightened. Be aware of things happening in secret and of possible deception. Control issue might arise. Forgive and forget. Avoid going to extremes.

- *Monday, March 28 (Moon into Sagittarius, 2:47 am)*
  It's as number 4 day. That means the emphasis today is on your organizational skills. In romance, your persistence pays off. You're building a foundation for the future. Control your impulses to wander off. Best to stay put and take care of your obligations. You could find missing papers now.

- *Tuesday, March 29 (Moon in Sagittarius)*
  With the moon in your first house today, you're sensitive to other people's feelings. You're malleable and easily change your mind. You may feel moody, withdrawn one moment, happy the next, then sad. Your self-awareness and appearance are important now. You're dealing with the person you are becoming.

- *Wednesday, March 30 (Moon into Capricorn, 1:46 pm)*
  It's a number 6 day, a service day. Be diplomatic, especially with someone who is giving you trouble. Do a good deed for someone. Visit someone who is ill or someone in need of help. Be sympathetic, kind, and compassionate, but avoid scattering your energies.

- *Thursday, March 31 (Moon in Capricorn)*
  The moon is in your second house today, boding well for financial matters. Look at your priorities in handling your income. Take care of payments and collect what's owed you. You equate your financial assets with emotional security now.

APRIL

- *Friday, April 1 (Moon into Aquarius, 9:38 pm)*
  It's a number 5 day. You're versatile and changeable today. Think outside the box. Take risks, experiment. Approach the day with an unconventional mindset. Get a new point of view. Your creativity, personal grace and magnetism are highlighted.

- *Saturday, April 2 (Moon in Aquarius)*
  The moon is in your third house today. You could be getting involved in some sort of aggressive mental activities, such as on-line gaming, a debate, or a game of chess, anything that challenges your mental prowess. If you're in school, you'll do great on tests now. Focus and expect success.

- *Sunday, April 3 (Moon in Aquarius)*
  Groups and social events are highlighted now. Your individuality is stressed. Your visionary abilities are heightened. You get a new perspective. You can bust old paradigms. Play your hunches. Look beyond the immediate.

- *Monday, April 4 (Moon into Pisces, 1:47 am)*
  It's a number 8 day, your power day. Unexpected money arrives. You're in the power seat so focus on a power play. You have a chance to expand, to gain recognition, fame, even power. It's a good day to buy a lotto ticket. Expect a windfall.

- *Tuesday, April 5 (Moon in Pisces)*
  Venus moves into your fifth house today and stays there until April 29. It's a great time for romance. You're particularly

attractive to the opposite sex now. It's also a good time for pursuing your creative talents, especially in the performing arts. Meanwhile, Mercury moves into your sixth house, indicating that you communicate well now with others in your workplace. It's also a good time to learn more about how you can improve your health and diet.

- *Wednesday, April 6 (Moon into Aries, 2:47 am)*
  It's a number 1 day and that means you're at the top of your cycle, Sadge. You get a fresh start, a new beginning. You can take the lead now, and don't be afraid to turn in a new direction. Stress originality in whatever you're doing.

- *Thursday, April 7 (Moon in Aries)*
  There's a new moon in your fifth house today. A new opportunity comes your way now related to a creative project and you love the way it sounds. It's a good time to begin a new project, possibly one involving children. Alternately, a new romance could be blossoming.

- *Friday, April 8 (Moon into Taurus, 2:11 am)*
  It's a number 3 day. Have fun today in preparation for tomorrow's discipline and focus. Make time to listen to others. Your charm and wit are appreciated. Spread your god news. You communicate well.

- *Saturday, April 9 (Moon in Taurus)*
  With the moon in your sixth house today, the emphasis turns to service to others. Help others, but don't deny your own needs. Be careful not to overlook any seemingly minor matters that could take on importance. Keep up with your exercise plan and watch your diet.

- *Sunday, April 10 (Moon into Gemini, 1:59 am)*
  It's a number 5 day. That means change and variety are highlighted now. Think freedom, think outside the box. No restrictions. Your creativity, personal grace and magnetism are highlighted.

- *Monday, April 11 (Moon in Gemini)*
The moon is in your seventh house today. You get along well with others now. You can fit in just about anywhere. Loved ones and partners are more important than usual. A legal matter could come to your attention. You comprehend the nuance of a situation, but it's difficult to go with the flow.

- *Tuesday, April 12 (Moon into Cancer, 2:07 am)*
It's a number 7 day, your mystery day. Secrets, intrigue, confidential information play a role today. You might feel best working on your own. You investigate, analyze or simply observe what's going on now. You quickly come to a conclusion and wonder why others don't see what you see. Don't make any final decisions until the new year, and take time to make some New Year's resolutions.

- *Wednesday, April 13 (Moon in Cancer)*
The moon is in your eighth house today. You could attract the attention of powerful people today. Your experiences could be more intense than usual, Sadge. Matters related to shared belongings, investments, taxes or insurance could play a role.

- *Thursday, April 14 (Moon into Leo, 9:54 am)*
It's a number 9 day. Finish what you've been working on and get ready for something new. But don't start anything today. Look beyond the immediate. Visualize the future; set your goals, then make them so. Express your desires, but avoid self-deception. Maintain your emotional balance.

- *Friday, April 15 (Moon in Leo)*
The moon is in your ninth house today. You're feeling as if you need to get away. Plan a trip or sign up for a seminar or workshop. A foreign country or person of foreign birth could play a role. Philosophy, religion, or mythology play a role in your day.

- *Saturday, April 16 (Moon into Virgo, 7:24 pm)*
It's a number 2 day. You could be undergoing some soul-searching related to a relationship now. Help comes through friends, loved

ones, especially a partner. Don't make waves. Don't rush or show resentment. Let things develop. The spotlight is on cooperation.

- *Sunday, April 17 (Moon in Virgo)*
  Pluto goes retrograde in your second house today, and stays that way until September 26. That means things get bogged down related to your finances. No matter how hard you try, it takes longer to achieve your financial goals. You tend to look inward more often and consider whether or not you're doing the right thing. Money issues are on your mind.

- *Monday, April 18 (Moon in Virgo)*
  With Mars now retrograde in your first house until late June, you face some delays in your personal life. The energy to pursue some personal issue is no longer there for you. You're less assertive over the next few weeks and tend to keep things to yourself rather than letting everyone know exactly what you think. Others might think you're hiding something.

- *Tuesday, April 19 (Moon into Libra, 7:25 am)*
  It's a number 5 day. Change and variety are highlighted now. Think freedom, no restrictions. Release old structures, get a new point of view. It's a good day to take a risk, experiment. Promote new ideas. Find a new point of view that fits current circumstances and what you know now.

- *Wednesday, April 20 (Moon in Libra)*
  The moon is in your eleventh house today. Friends play an important role in your day, especially Aries and Leo. You find strength in numbers, and meaning through friends and groups. Social consciousness plays a role.

- *Thursday, April 21 (Moon into Scorpio, 8:19 pm)*
  There's a full moon in your twelfth house today. Now you can reap what you've sown. You gain a better understanding of matters from the past. An institution, such as a hospital, prison or government office could play a role. However, it's best to work behind the scenes today.

- *Friday, April 22 (Moon in Scorpio)*
  With the moon remaining in your twelfth house, yesterday's energy flows into your Friday. Unconscious attitudes can be difficult. So can relations with women. Keep your feelings to yourself now. Be aware of hidden enemies. It's a great day for a mystical or spiritual discipline. Your intuition is heightened.

- *Saturday, April 23 (Moon in Scorpio)*
  You could be exploring and developing psychic talents now. You investigate, research, and dig deep. Be aware of things happening in secret and of possible deception. Expect intense, emotional experiences today. You're passionate and your sexuality is heightened. Forgive and forget, try to avoid going to extremes.

- *Sunday, April 24 (Moon into Sagittarius, 8:47 am)*
  It's a number 1 day and you're at the top of your cycle. Get out and meet new people, have new experiences, do something you've never done before. You're inspired to turn your career in a new direction. Don't fear change. In romance, a flirtation turns more serious.

- *Monday, April 25 (Moon in Sagittarius)*
  The moon is on your ascendant today, Sadge. The way you see yourself now is the way others see you. You're feeling recharged, and this makes you more appealing to the public. You're physically vital, and relations with the opposite sex go well.

- *Tuesday, April 26 (Moon into Capricorn, 7:55 pm)*
  It's a number 3 day. Take time to relax, enjoy yourself, recharge your batteries. You can influence people now with your upbeat attitude. Your charm and wit are appreciated. Foster generosity. In romance, you're an ardent lover and loyal.

- *Wednesday, April 27 (Moon in Capricorn)*
  The moon is in your second house today. Expect emotional experiences related to money. You identify emotionally with your possessions or whatever you value. Look at your priorities in handling your income. Put off making any major purchases now.

• *Thursday, April 28 (Moon in Capricorn)*
Mercury goes retrograde in your sixth house and stays there until May 22. That means you can expect some glitches and delays in your daily work over the next three weeks. There also could be delays related to short distance travel, and some confusion about a health issue. Keep in mind that things will become much clearer later next month.

• *Friday, April 29 (Moon into Aquarius, 4:47 am)*
Venus moves into your sixth house today, and that softens the impact of Mercury retrograde that began yesterday. It's a good time to pursue an office romance, if that's what you want. Your work environment is harmonious, especially if you're working on a creative project now. You enjoy helping others and are rewarded for your efforts. Your health picture is looking good.

• *Saturday, April 30 (Moon in Aquarius)*
The moon is in your third house today. You can be quite opinionated today, especially when talking with siblings, family members or neighbors. Try to stay in control of your emotions. You tend to be affected by matters from the past. Best to let go of those old issues.

MAY

- *Sunday, May 1 (Moon into Pisces, 10:34 am)*
  It's a number 6 day. Service to others is the theme of the day. You offer advice and support. Be diplomatic toward anyone complaining or criticizing now. Try to make people happy. Be sympathetic, kind, and compassionate. But avoid scattering your energies.

- *Monday, May 2 (Moon in Pisces)*
  The moon is in your fourth house today, Sadge. Spend time with your family and loved ones. Stick close to home, and work on a project to beautify your home. You could be dealing with parents now. You feel a close tie to your roots.

- *Tuesday, May 3 (Moon into Aries, 1:05 pm)*
  It's a number 8 day, your power day. Unexpected money arrives. You're in the power seat so focus on a power play. You have a chance to expand, to gain recognition, fame, even power. It's a good day to buy a lotto ticket. Expect a windfall.

- *Wednesday, May 4 (Moon in Aries)*
  The moon is in your fifth house today. You're emotionally in touch with your creative side. It's a good day to take a chance, experiment. Be aware that your emotions tend to overpower your intellect. Alternately, you are more protective and nurturing toward children.

- *Thursday, May 5 (Moon into Taurus, 1:11 pm)*
  It's a number 1 day and you're at the top of your cycle. Independence

is the theme today. Don't be afraid to turn in a new direction. You're inventive and make connections that others overlook. Trust your hunches. You get a fresh start, a new beginning.

- *Friday, May 6 (Moon in Taurus)*
  There's a new moon in your sixth house today. That means new opportunities come your way related to service. Help others, but don't deny your own needs. Be careful not to overlook any seemingly minor matters that could take on importance. Keep up with your exercise plan and watch your diet.

- *Saturday, May 7 (Moon into Gemini, 12:35 pm)*
  It's a number 3 day. Your attitude determines everything today, Sadge. You communicate well now. You're curious and inventive. Ideas bubble forth. Your imagination is keen now. Your popularity is on the rise.

- *Sunday, May 8 (Moon in Gemini)*
  With the moon is your seventh house today, lovers and partners are highlighted. Your emotions are more intense, Sadge. Women play a prominent role in your day. You feel a need to be accepted. You're looking for security, but you have a hard time going with the flow. A legal matter comes to a head now.

- *Monday, May 9, (Moon into Cancer, 1:25 pm)*
  Jupiter goes direct in your tenth house today. Career or professional matters occupy your attention. You have a chance to grow and expand whatever you're doing. Co-workers play an important role. You could make money now through a publishing project.

- *Tuesday, May 10 (Moon in Cancer)*
  The moon is in your eighth house today. Take care of any matters related to taxes, insurance or investments. Be aware that emotions can get intense now, especially when dealing with shared resources. You could take an interest in a metaphysical topic now, such as life after death or past lives.

- *Wednesday, May 11 (Moon into Leo, 5:33 pm)*
  It's a number 7 day, a mystery day. You keep an eye on what's going on around you. You quickly come to a conclusion and wonder why others don't see what you see. You work best on your own today. Make sure that you see things as they are, not as you wish them to be. Knowledge is essential to success.

- *Thursday, May 12 (Moon in Leo)*
  The moon is in your ninth house today, you native home, Sadge. You're captivated by new ideas and philosophies. You're a dreamer and a thinker. You may feel a need to get away now, a break from the usual routine. You're feeling restless and yearn for a new experience.

- *Friday, May 13 (Moon in Leo)*
  Theatrics and drama are highlighted. You're at center stage today. Be wild, imaginative, be the person you always imagined you might be. Play with different personas, flaunt and celebrate. Romance feels majestic.

- *Saturday, May 14 (Moon into Virgo, 00:53 am)*
  It's a number 1 day. Take the lead, get a fresh start, a new beginning. Don't be afraid to turn in a new direction. Trust your hunches. Your intuition is highlighted. Stress originality in whatever you're doing. You attract creative people now. In romance, a flirtation turns more serious.

- *Sunday, May 15 (Moon in Virgo)*
  The moon is in your tenth house today. Your life is more public today. You're more responsive to the needs and moods of a group and of the public in general. Avoid any emotional displays in public, such as at a company gathering.

- *Monday, May 16 (Moon into Libra, 1:34 pm)*
  It's a number 3 day. Have fun today in preparation for tomorrow's discipline and focus. Make time to listen to others. Your charm and wit are appreciated. Spread your god news. You communicate well.

- *Tuesday, May 17 (Moon in Libra)*
  The moon is in your eleventh house today. You get along better with friends and associates. You join a group of like-minded individuals and work for the common good. Your interests are so diverse now, Sadge, that others might think you lack depth. Your sense of security is tied to your relationships and to your friends.

- *Wednesday, May 18 (Moon in Libra)*
  Romance is highlighted. Relationships issues figure prominently in your day. It's a good day for going to a concert, an art gallery opening, the theater. Feed your creative juices. Your personal grace and magnetism are emphasized.

- *Thursday, May 19 (Moon into Scorpio, 2:31 am)*
  It's a number 6 day. That means diplomacy is called for in all your interactions. You offer support and advice, but take time to dance to your own tune! Be understanding and avoid confrontations.

- *Friday, May 20 (Moon in Scorpio)*
  The moon is in your twelfth house today. Best to work behind the scenes today and avoid any conflicts and confrontations, especially with women. Keep your feelings secret. Unconscious attitudes can be difficult.

- *Saturday, May 21 (Moon into Sagittarius, 2:49 pm)*
  There's a full moon in your first house, which suggests that you gain insight into a health issue or another personal matter. Your appearance and self-awareness becomes more acute as you realize that you reap what you've sown. You're dealing with the person you are becoming.

- *Sunday, May 22 (Moon in Sagittarius)*
  Mercury moves into your sixth house today. You're methodical and thorough in your approach to work over the next three weeks. You make sure everything is just right. You're efficient and capable, but you can get flustered easily by disorder. You also might be overly concerned about your health and diet.

- *Monday, May 23 (Moon in Sagittarius)*
  The moon is on your ascendant as the week begins. That means your face is in front of the public. You're feeling recharged for the rest of the year. Your appearance and personality are vibrant. You feelings and thoughts are aligned today. It's your day to shine.

- *Tuesday, May 24 (Moon into Capricorn, 1:34 am)*
  Venus moves into your seventh house today. You and your partner or friends get along well now. A marriage or partnership brings success and prosperity. You can fit in just about anywhere.

- *Wednesday, May 25 (Moon in Capricorn)*
  The moon moves into your second house today. Expect emotional experiences related to money. You identify emotionally with your possessions or whatever you value. It's not the objects themselves that are important, rather it's the feeling you hold related to them. Take care of any payments and collect what's owed you.

- *Thursday, May 26 (Moon into Aquarius, 10:27 am)*
  It's a number 4 day. Be practical with your money. Persevere to get things done today, and don't get sloppy. Control your impulses. Take care of your obligations. You're building foundations for an outlet for your creativity.

- *Friday, May 27 (Moon in Aquarius)*
  The moon is in your third house today. Expect a lot of running around today, short trips here and there. After all, you're dealing with the everyday world. Try to group things together to cut down on your trips. You could have contact with neighbors or siblings today. Be careful talking on your cell and driving.

- *Saturday, May 28 (Moon into Pisces, 5:06 pm)*
  It's a number 6 day. Service to others is the theme of the day. Be diplomatic to anyone complaining or criticizing now. Try to make people happy. Be sympathetic, kind, and compassionate. Offer advice and support, but avoid scattering your energies.

- *Sunday, May 29 (Moon in Pisces)*

  The moon is in your fourth house. You're dealing with your home life and the foundations of who you are. Spend time at home with family and loved ones. It's a good day to beautify your home. Spend some time in meditation.

- *Monday, May 30 (Moon into Aries, 9:10 pm)*

  It's a number 8 day, your power day. Unexpected money arrives. You're in the power seat so focus on a power play. You have a chance to expand, to gain recognition, fame, even power. It's a good day to buy a lotto ticket. Expect a windfall.

- *Tuesday, May 31 (Moon in Aries)*

  The moon is in your fifth house today. You're emotionally in touch with your creative side now. It's a good day to take a chance, experiment. Be aware that your emotions tend to overpower your intellect. Alternately, you are more protective and nurturing toward children.

JUNE

- **Wednesday, June 1, (Moon into Taurus, 10:48 pm)**
  It's a number 7 day. You're launching a journey into the unknown. Knowledge is essential to success. You're a spy for your own cause today. Go with the flow. Maintain your emotional balance, and don't make any absolute decisions until tomorrow.

- **Thursday, June 2 (Moon in Taurus)**
  The moon is in your sixth house today. It's a service day. You're the one others go to for help. Keep your resolutions about exercise and watch your diet. Attend to details related to your health. Make a doctor or dentist appointment. Your personal health occupies your attention now.

- **Friday, June 3 (Moon into Gemini, 11:03 pm)**
  It's a number 9 day. Visualize for the future, and strive for universal appeal. Set your goals, then make them so. You're up to the challenge. Complete a project and get ready for something new that's coming up.

- **Saturday, June 4 (Moon in Gemini)**
  There's a new moon in your seventh house today. You get a new opportunity now and could be negotiating or signing a contract now. You're taking the initiative with your partner, and emotions could get volatile. It's difficult to maintain an objective and detached point of view. Be careful not to let others manipulate your feelings.

- *Sunday, June 5 (Moon into Cancer, 11:43 pm)*
  It's a number 2 day. The spotlight shines on cooperative efforts.
  If you're married, your marriage takes on more significance and
  brings in more structure to your life. If you're not married, there
  could be some soul-searching related to a relationship, or a new
  relationship developing. Help comes through friends today.

- *Monday , June 6 (Moon in Cancer)*
  The moon is in your eighth house today. You could attract the
  attention of powerful people today. Your experiences could
  be more intense than usual, Sadge. Matters related to shared
  belongings, investments, taxes or insurance could play a role.

- *Tuesday, June 7 (Moon in Cancer)*
  You could feel moody today and overly sensitive. Keep things
  to yourself and don't allow other people's moods to bring you
  down. Get out and take a walk. You might feel a need to be near
  water.

- *Wednesday, June 8 (Moon into Leo, 2:48 am)*
  It's a number 5 day. Variety is the spice of life. Think freedom, no
  restrictions. Promote new ideas, follow your curiosity. Look for
  adventure. Think outside the box. You can overcome obstacles
  with ease.

- *Thursday, June 9 (Moon in Leo)*
  The moon is in your ninth house today. You're captivated by
  new ideas and philosophies. You're a dreamer and a thinker.
  You may feel a need to get away now, a break from the usual
  routine. You're feeling restless and yearn for a new experience.

- *Friday, June 10 (Moon into Virgo, 9:47 am)*
  It's a number 7 day, a mystery day. Keep an eye on what's going
  on around you. You quickly come to a conclusion and wonder
  why others don't see what you see. You work best on your own
  today. Make sure that you see things as they are, not as you wish
  them to be. Knowledge is essential to success.

- *Saturday, June 11 (Moon in Virgo)*
  The moon is in your tenth house today. You're either gaining a boost in status, recognition and personal achievement, or you're feeling in need of the same now. You find yourself more in the public, but try to avoid any overly emotional displays.

- *Sunday, June 12, (Moon into Libra, 8:34 pm)*
  With Mercury moving into your seventh house, you tend to spend time with creative, witty, and well-spoken people now. You feel a need to communicate with knowledgeable and intelligent people. You get along well with others and can resolve any disagreements.

- *Monday, June 13 (Moon in Libra)*
  The moon is in your eleventh house today. Friends play an important role in your day, especially Aries and Leo. You work well with a group and find strength in numbers, especially if you're with a group of like-minded people working for the common good.

- *Tuesday, June 14 (Moon in Libra)*
  You can keep everyone in balance around you today, Sadge. Relationships issues figure prominently. Feed your creative juices. It's a good day for going to a concert, an art gallery opening, the theater. Your personal grace and magnetism are emphasized. Romance is highlighted.

- *Wednesday, June 15 (Moon into Scorpio, 9:19 am)*
  It's a number 3 day. Have fun today in preparation for tomorrow's discipline and focus. Make time to listen to others. Your charm and wit are appreciated. Spread your good news. You communicate well.

- *Thursday, June 16 (Moon in Scorpio)*
  The moon is in your twelfth house today. It's a great day for a mystical or spiritual discipline. Your intuition is heightened. Unconscious attitudes can be difficult now. So can relations with women. Keep your feelings secret. Follow your intuition.

- *Friday, June 17 (Moon into Sagittarius, 9:34 pm)*
  Venus moves into your eighth house today. You can gain financially now through a marriage or any type of partnership. Things might seem easy now, but don't just lay back. Promote new ideas, follow your curiosity. Approach the day with an unconventional mindset.

- *Saturday, June 18 (Moon in Sagittarius)*
  The moon is on your ascendant. Your appearance and personality shines. You feelings and thoughts are aligned today. Your face is in front of the public, and you get along well with others.

- *Sunday, June 19 (Moon in Sagittarius)*
  You're a dreamer and a thinker, Sadge. You yearn for a new experience. Plan a long trip or sign up for a workshop or seminar. In romance, a friend could introduce you to someone new and exciting from far away.

- *Monday, June 20 (Moon into Capricorn, 7:55 am)*
  There's a full moon in your second house today. You reap what you've sown now related finances. You gain insight, a new perspective on personal financial matters and also your values, or whatever you value.

- *Tuesday, June 21 (Moon in Capricorn)*
  With the moon remaining in your second house today, you feel best now surrounded by familiar objects, your stuff. It's not the objects themselves that are important, but the feelings and memories you associate with them. Put off making any major purchases for at least a day or two. You equate your financial assets with emotional security now.

- *Wednesday, June 22 (Moon into Aquarius, 4:09 pm)*
  It's a number 1 day so you're at the top of your cycle again. You take the lead, Sadge, and get a fresh start. Don't be afraid to turn in a new direction. You attract creative people. Stress originality.

- *Thursday, June 23 (Moon in Aquarius)*
  The moon is in your third house today. Your communications with others are subjective. Take what you know and share it with others, but control your emotions. That's especially true when dealing with siblings and relatives, or neighbors. Your thinking is unduly influenced by things from the past.

- *Friday, June 24 (Moon into Pisces, 10:31 pm)*
  It's a number 3 day. You're warm and receptive to what others say. Your imagination is keen now. You're curious and inventive. Enjoy the harmony, beauty and pleasures of life. Overall, the social energy of the day is warm and welcoming. Your popularity is on the rise.

- *Saturday, June 25 (Moon in Pisces)*
  With the moon in your fourth house, emotional issues arise related to the domestic scene. You could be feeling possessive of loved ones. It's a good day to retreat to a private place for quiet meditation. Find a new way to beautify your home scene.

- *Sunday, June 26 (Moon in Pisces)*
  It's a day for deep healing. Imagination is highlighted. Watch for psychic events, synchronicities. Keep track of your dreams, including your daydreams. Ideas are ripe. You can tap deeply into the collective unconscious for inspiration.

- *Monday, June 27 (Moon into Aries, 3:09 am)*
  It's a number 6 day, a service day. Adjust to the needs of loved ones. You serve, teach, and guide. But know when to say enough is enough. Clear up a situation at home that has lingered too long. Be understanding and avoid confrontations.

- *Tuesday, June 28 (Moon in Aries)*
  With the moon is in your fifth house today, you're emotionally in touch with your creative side now. Be yourself. Be emotionally honest. In love, there's greater emotional depth to a relationship. You might be somewhat possessive of loved ones now, particularly children.

- *Wednesday, June 29 (Moon into Taurus, 6:05 am)*
  Mercury moves into your eighth house today. You take a renewed interest in matters of life and death, and what comes afterwards. You investigate and dig deep. While you may read an interesting book on the subject, much of what you conclude comes through your intuition.

- *Thursday, June 30 (Moon in Taurus)*
  The moon is in your sixth house today. Exercise and diet play a role today. Attend to details related to your health. Make a doctor or dentist appointment. Help others, but don't deny your own needs. Friends play a role today, Sadge. Meet them at the gym.

JULY

- **Friday, July 1 (*Moon into Gemini, 6:46 am*)**
  You have a chance to expand, to gain recognition, even fame and power. You attract financial success, especially if you open your mind to a new approach. You're playing with power so be careful not to hurt others. Business discussions go well.

- **Saturday, July 2 (*Moon in Gemini*)**
  The moon is in your seventh house today. Cooperation is highlighted. Don't make waves; just go with the flow today. Loved ones and partners are more important than usual. Look for ways to expand whatever you're doing, and make sure you explain your plans to others who are affected.

- **Sunday, July 3 (*Moon into Cancer, 8:21 am*)**
  It's a number 1 day and you're at the top of your cycle again. Stress originality now as you get a fresh start. Get out and meet new people, have new experiences, do something you've never done before. Don't be afraid to turn in a new direction. Trust your hunches. You're inventive and make connections that others overlook. You're determined and courageous today.

- **Monday, July 4 (*Moon in Cancer*)**
  There's a new moon in your eighth house today. That means new opportunities come your way related to shared possessions. That could mean an inheritance, insurance or legal settlement. Alternately, you pursue new options related to your interest in mystical matters. Watch for synchronicities, Sadge.

- *Tuesday, July 5 (Moon into Leo, 11:29 am)*
  It's a number 3 day. Your attitude determines everything today, Sadge. You communicate well now. You're curious and inventive. Ideas bubble forth. Your imagination is keen now. Your popularity is on the rise.

- *Wednesday, July 6 (Moon in Leo)*
  The moon is in your ninth house today, your native home, Sadge. You're captivated by new ideas and philosophies. You're a dreamer and a thinker. You may feel a need to get away now, a break from the usual routine. You're feeling restless and yearn for a new experience.

- *Thursday, July 7 (Moon into Virgo, 5:42 pm)*
  It's a number 5 day. You're versatile and changeable today. Think outside the box. Take risks, experiment. Approach the day with an unconventional mindset. Get a new point of view.

- *Friday, July 8 (Moon in Virgo)*
  The moon is in your tenth house today and that means professional concerns take priority. After your positive day yesterday, you could gain favor from bosses or the public. It's a good day for sales, dealing with the public. You're more responsive to the needs of others, especially co-workers.

- *Saturday, July 9 (Moon in Virgo)*
  Stick close to home, focus on tidying up the house, attend to the detail and loose ends. You may exhibit some perfectionist tendencies now. Relax. Take time to write in a journal. You write from a deep place now with lots of details and colorful descriptions.

- *Sunday, July 10 (Moon into Libra, 3:33 am)*
  It's a number 8 day, your power day. You're confident and material success is within reach if not already here. You attract financial success. You're playing with power so be careful not to hurt others. Be courageous and honest.

- *Monday, July 11 (Moon in Libra)*
The moon is in your eleventh house today, Sadge. Your friendships expand now as new people come into your life. You find strength in numbers, and meaning through friends and groups. Focus on your wishes and dreams. Examine your overall goals. Those goals should be an expression of who you are.

- *Tuesday, July 12 (Moon into Scorpio, 3:53 pm)*
Venus moves into your ninth house today. You love the idea of distant travel and this month is a good time for planning such a trip, or taking one, if possible. A love affair with a foreign-born person could develop now.

- *Wednesday, July 13 (Moon in Scorpio)*
Mercury joins Venus in your ninth house today. You're actively discussing ideas now that could involve a foreign destination or a person of foreign origin. A long trip, possibly in pursuit of higher education, is on your mind. You also communicate your ideas about philosophy, mythology or religion. You're physically vital, and relations with the opposite sex go well.

- *Thursday, July 14 (Moon in Scorpio)*
The moon is in your twelfth house today. Unconscious attitudes can be difficult now. So can relations with women. Keep your feelings secret unless you're confiding in a close friend. You might feel a need to withdraw and spend a few hours by yourself. Take time to reflect and meditate.

- *Friday, July 15 (Moon into Sagittarius, 4:15 am)*
It's a number 4 day. Your organizational skills are highlighted now, but try not to wander off task. Emphasize quality. You're building a creative foundation for your future. Tear down the old in order to rebuild. Be methodical and thorough.

- *Saturday, July 16 (Moon in Sagittarius)*
The moon moves into your first house today. Your self-awareness or appearance is important now, Sadge. You're dealing with the

person you are becoming. You may feel moody, withdrawn one moment, happy the next, then sad. It's all about your emotional self. Your feelings and thoughts are aligned.

- *Sunday, July 17 (Moon into Capricorn, 2:34 pm)*
  It's a number 6 day. Focus on making people happy today. Be sympathetic, kind, and compassionate. Do a good deed for someone. But avoid scattering your energy. Dance to your own tune.

- *Monday, July 18 (Moon in Capricorn)*
  The moon is in your second house today. Expect emotional experiences related to money and your values. It's a good day for investments, but be practical. Don't make any major purchases now. You seek financial and domestic security now, and you feel best surrounded by familiar objects now.

- *Tuesday, July 19 (Moon into Aquarius, 10:12 pm)*
  There's a full moon in your third house today. You learn something about your siblings, relatives or neighbors today that shed new light on a situation. You have an emotional need now to dig into something from the past. You reap what you've sown.

- *Wednesday, July 20 (Moon in Aquarius)*
  The moon is in your third house today. You could be getting involved in some sort of aggressive mental activities, such as on-line gaming, a debate, or a game of chess, anything that challenges your mental prowess. If you're in school, you'll do great on tests now.

- *Thursday, July 21 (Moon in Aquarius)*
  Groups and social events are highlighted now. Your individuality is stressed. Your visionary abilities are heightened. You get a new perspective. You can bust old paradigms. Play your hunches. Look beyond the immediate.

- *Friday, July 22 (Moon into Pisces, 3:37 am)*
  It's a number 2 day. Use your intuition to get a sense of your day. Be kind and understanding. Cooperation, especially with

partners, is highlighted. Don't make waves. Don't rush or show resentment. Let things develop. Marriage plays a key role.

- *Saturday, July 23 (Moon in Pisces)*
  The moon is in your fourth house today, Sadge. Spend time with your family and loved ones. Stick close to home, and work on a project to beautify your home. You could be dealing with parents now. You feel a close tie to your roots.

- *Sunday, July 24 (Moon into Aries, 7:34 am)*
  It's a number 4 day. Control your impulses. Stay grounded today. Romance takes a back burner. Take care of your obligations. Remain focused and you can solve any problem you face.

- *Monday, July 25 (Moon in Aries)*
  The moon is in your fifth house today. Your love life takes off now. There's an idealistic turn to whatever you do for pleasure. It's a great time for a creative project, especially fiction writing. You could be somewhat possessive of loved ones and children today.

- *Tuesday, July 26 (Moon into Taurus, 10:38 am)*
  It's a number 6 day. Service to others is the theme of the day, and diplomacy wins the way. Do a good deed for someone. Visit someone who is ill or someone in need of help. Focus on making people happy. A domestic adjustment works out for the best.

- *Wednesday, July 27 (Moon in Taurus)*
  The moon is in your sixth house today. Exercise and diet play a role today. Attend to details related to your health. Make a doctor or dentist appointment. Help others, but don't deny your own needs. Friends play a role today, Sadge. Meet them at the gym. You get a fresh start.

- *Thursday, July 28 (Moon into Gemini, 1:17 pm)*
  It's a number 8 day, your power day, and your day to play it your way. Think big and act big! Unexpected money arrives. You have a chance to expand, to gain recognition, even fame and power.

- *Friday, July 29 (Moon in Gemini)*
  Uranus goes retrograde in your fifth house today and stays that way until Dec. 17. That means you might be doing some soul-searching about a creative project. You could be getting flashes of inspiration. You also might be more accident prone over the next few months. Watch your step!

- *Saturday, July 30 (Moon into Cancer, 4:09 pm)*
  Mercury moving into your tenth house today. That means communication skills are essential now in your career. You could also be traveling for business during the next two to three weeks. You get along with co-workers and get our ideas across.

- *Sunday, July 31 (Moon in Cancer)*
  The moon is in your eighth house today. Your experiences are more intense than usual today. You have a strong sense of duty and feel obligated to fulfill your promises. You also could be exploring metaphysical ideas now, possibly past lives, hauntings, or life after death.

AUGUST

- *Monday, August 1 (Moon into Leo, 8:12 pm)*
  It's a number 9 day. Complete a project now. Clear up odds and ends. Take an inventory on where things are going in your life. It's a good day to make a donation to a worthy cause. Use the day for reflection, expansion, and concluding projects, but don't start anything new today.

- *Tuesday, August 2 (Moon in Leo)*
  Mars moves into your first house today, and stays there until September 27. You're going to be more outgoing, more aggressive as you pursue your ideas. You want others to take notice, even if they don't agree. There's also a new moon in your ninth house today. That means you could gain a new opportunity now related to higher education or long-distance travel. You're in the driver's seat.

- *Wednesday, August 3 (Moon in Leo)*
  The moon remains in your ninth house today. Your mind is active and you yearn for new experiences, a break from the routine, a change from the status quo. You can create positive change through your ideas now. A publishing project takes off. Publicity and advertising are emphasized.

- *Thursday, August 4 (Moon into Virgo, 2:34 am)*
  It's a number 3 day. Your attitude determines everything today, Sadge. You communicate well now. You're curious and inventive. Ideas bubble forth. Your imagination is keen now. Enjoy the harmony, beauty and pleasures of life.

- *Friday, August 5 (Moon in Virgo)*
  Venus moves into your tenth house today, giving you a greater love and appreciation of your profession. You have a strong yearning to move ahead in your career. You're visible to the public now and things are picking up in your career. You do exceptionally well in a large organization now. It's a good time for coming up with money-making ideas.

- *Saturday, August 6 (Moon into Libra,11:57 am)*
  It's a number 5 day. Variety is the spice of life. Think freedom, no restrictions. Promote new ideas, follow your curiosity. Look for adventure. Think outside the box. You can overcome obstacles with ease.

- *Sunday, August 7 (Moon in Libra)*
  The moon is in your eleventh house today. Friends play an important role in your day, especially Aries and Leo, and you take the initiative to get together with them. You find strength in numbers, and meaning through friends and groups. Social consciousness plays a role.

- *Monday, August 8 (Moon into Scorpio, 11:52 pm)*
  It's a number 7 day, a mystery day. You keep an eye on what's going on around you. You quickly come to a conclusion and wonder why others don't see what you see. You work best on your own today. Make sure that you see things as they are, not as you wish them to be. Knowledge is essential to success.

- *Tuesday, August 9 (Moon in Scorpio)*
  The moon is in your twelfth house today. Think carefully before you act today. There's a tendency now to undo all the positive actions you've taken in recent days. You're more sensitive than usual today, Sadge. Avoid any self-destructive tendencies. Best to back off now rather than confront a suspected enemy. Hide your emotions. Keep your feelings secret.

• *Wednesday, August 10 (Moon in Scorpio)*
Secrets, intrigue, confidential information play a role. You work best on your own today. Knowledge is essential to success. Gather information, but don't make any absolute decisions until tomorrow. Go with the flow.

• *Thursday, August 11 (Moon into Sagittarius, 12:26 pm)*
It's a number 1 day. Take the lead, get a fresh start, a new beginning. Don't be afraid to turn in a new direction. Trust your hunches. Your intuition is highlighted. Stress originality in whatever you're doing. You attract creative people now. In romance, a flirtation turns more serious.

• *Friday, August 12 (Moon in Sagittarius)*
The moon is on your ascendant today. The way you see yourself is the way others see you now. You could be seeing two sides to your personality. You're also more in the public view today than earlier in the week. You're recharged for the rest of the month and this makes you more appealing to others. You're physically vital, and relations with the opposite sex go well.

• *Saturday, August 13 (Moon into Capricorn, 11:13 pm)*
It's a number 3 day. Your attitude determines everything today. You communicate well. You're warm and receptive to what others say. Ease up on routines. Remain flexible. Enjoy the harmony, beauty and pleasures of life.

• *Sunday, August 14 (Moon in Capricorn)*
The moon is in your second house today, boding well for financial matters. Look at your priorities in handling your income. Take care of payments and collect what's owed you. You equate your financial assets with emotional security now.

• *Monday, August 15 (Moon in Capricorn)*
Your ambition and drive to succeed are highlighted. Your responsibilities increase. You may feel stressed and overworked, but don't ignore your exercise routine. Authority figures or elderly people play a role.

- *Tuesday, August 16 (Moon into Aquarius, 6:54 am)*
  It's a number 6 day, a service day. Diplomacy is called for now. Be sympathetic and kind, generous and tolerant. Focus on making people happy. Do a good deed for someone, but dance to your own tune.

- *Wednesday, August 17 (Moon in Aquarius)*
  The moon is in your third house today. Expect a lot of running around today, short trips here and there. After all, you're dealing with the everyday world. Try to group things together to cut down on your trips. You could have contact with neighbors or siblings today. Be careful talking on your cell and driving.

- *Thursday, August 18 (Moon into Pisces, 11:35 am)*
  There's a full moon in your third house today. You learn something about your siblings, relatives or neighbors today that shed new light on a situation better. You have an emotional need now to dig into something from the past. You reap what you've sown.

- *Friday, August 19 (Moon in Pisces)*
  The moon is in your fourth house today. Spend time with your family and loved ones. Stick close to home, if possible today. You feel a close tie to your roots. You're dealing with the foundations of who you are and who you are becoming. A parent plays a role.

- *Saturday, August 20 (Moon into Aries, 2:19 pm)*
  It's a number 1 day and you're at the top of your cycle. Now it's time to take the lead. Independence is the theme today. You're inventive and make connections that others overlook. Trust your hunches. You get a fresh start, a new beginning.

- *Sunday, August 21 (Moon in Aries)*
  The moon is in your fifth house today. You're emotionally in touch with your creative side now. It's a good day to take a chance, experiment. Be aware that your emotions tend to overpower your intellect. Alternately, you are more protective and nurturing toward children.

- *Monday, August 22 (Moon into Taurus, 4:20 pm)*
It's a number 3 day. Your attitude determines everything today, Sadge. You communicate well now. You're curious and inventive. Ideas bubble forth. Your imagination is keen now. Your popularity is on the rise.

- *Tuesday, August 23 (Moon in Taurus)*
With the moon in your sixth house today, the emphasis turns to your daily work and health. Look for ways to communicate better with those in your workplace, Sadge. Offer your services to those who see you as the one with the answers and abilities. Don't forget to stick with your exercise plan.

- *Wednesday, August 24 (Moon into Gemini, 6:40 pm)*
It's a number 5 day. Variety is the spice of life. Think freedom, no restrictions. Promote new ideas, follow your curiosity. Look for adventure. Think outside the box. You can overcome obstacles with ease.

- *Thursday, August 25 (Moon in Gemini)*
The moon is in your seventh house today. It's a great time for creating a new partnership or enhancing an old one, whether it's personal or business-oriented. You prosper in any partnership now. You're friendly and affectionate with loved ones.

- *Friday, August 26 (Moon into Cancer, 10:07 pm)*
It's a number 7 day, a mystery day. You keep an eye on what's going on around you. You quickly come to a conclusion and wonder why others don't see what you see. You work best on your own today. Make sure that you see things as they are, not as you wish them to be. Knowledge is essential to success.

- *Saturday, August 27 (Moon in Cancer)*
The moon is in your eighth house today. You attract the attention of powerful people. You could be dealing with a matter related to shared belongings, investments, or taxes. An interest in metaphysics plays a role. You could be reading about concepts of life after death or reincarnation. Be aware that your experiences could be more intense than usual.

- *Sunday, August 28 (Moon in Cancer)*
  Your home and your personal environment take on more importance today. Don't allow other people's moods to bring you down. Get out and take a walk. Do something to beautify your home. You're intuitive and nurturing now.

- *Monday, August 29 (Moon into Leo, 3:12 am)*
  Venus moves into your eleventh house today. A new romance could spark now with one of your colleagues or someone you work with in a group. A relationship now furthers your wishes and dreams.

- *Tuesday, August 30 (Moon in Leo)*
  Mercury goes retrograde in your tenth house today and stays there until September 22. There could be some miscommunication and misunderstanding about what you're doing in the workplace. Career issues arise, and you need to make sure that you are understood. Expect delays and glitches in your plans, but don't worry it won't last.

- *Wednesday, August 31 (Moon into Virgo, 10:23 am)*
  It's a number 3 day. Your attitude determines everything today, Sadge. You're curious and inventive. Ideas bubble forth. Your imagination is keen now. Your popularity is on the rise.

SEPTEMBER

- *Thursday, September 1 (Moon in Virgo)*
  There's a solar eclipse today in your tenth house. Expect new opportunities related to your career to come your way very rapidly. Co-workers are supportive and helpful. You stand out in the public eye and gain a notable elevation in prestige.

- *Friday, September 2 (Moon into Libra, 7:57 pm)*
  It's a number 2 day. Focus more on relationships today. Cooperation and partnerships are emphasized. Use your intuition when dealing with others. You're ambitious in pursuing a partnership. You excel in working with others now.

- *Saturday, September 3 (Moon in Libra)*
  The moon is in your eleventh house today. You work well with a group today, especially if the members are of like mind. Friends play an important role. Focus on your wishes and dreams and make sure that they're still compatible with your interests.

- *Sunday, September 4 (Moon in Libra)*
  Romance is highlighted. Relationships issues figure prominently in your day. Museums, art, music, creativity all figure in. It's a day for feeding your creative juices. In romance, it's a good time to schedule an amorous adventure.

- *Monday, September 5 (Moon into Scorpio, 7:40 am)*
  It's a number 5 day. That means it's a good day to promote new ideas. You're versatile, changeable. Be careful not to spread out and diversify too much. Freedom of thought and action are key. A change of scenery would work to your advantage.

- *Tuesday, September 6 (Moon in Scorpio)*
  The moon is in your twelfth house today. Think carefully before you act today. There's a tendency now to undo all the positive actions you've taken. You're more sensitive than usual today, Sadge. Best to work behind the scenes rather than confront a suspected enemy.

- *Wednesday, September 7 (Moon into Sagittarius, 8:21 pm)*
  It's a number 7 day today. Get ready for a journey into the unknown. Secrets, intrigue, confidential information play a role. Knowledge is essential to success. Gather information, but don't make any absolute decisions until tomorrow. You work best on your own today.

- *Thursday, September 8 (Moon in Sagittarius)*
  The moon is on your ascendant today. The way you see yourself now is the way others see you. You're feeling recharged and ready to go. You're physically vital, and relations with the opposite sex go well. Your appearance and personality shines.

- *Friday, September 9 (Moon in Sagittarius)*
  Jupiter moves into your eleventh house today in a major transit that should over the coming months have a positive effect on your efforts to achieve your wishes and dreams. New opportunities to expand whatever you're doing come through your relationship with a group of like-minded people. You have deeper contact with friends now.

- *Saturday, September 10 (Moon into Capricorn, 7:56 am)*
  It's a number 1 day. Take the lead, get a fresh start, a new beginning. Don't be afraid to turn in a new direction. Trust your hunches. Your intuition is highlighted. Stress originality in whatever you're doing. You attract creative people now. In romance, a flirtation turns more serious.

- *Sunday, September 11 (Moon in Capricorn)*
  The moon is in your second house today. You identify emotionally with your possessions or whatever you value. It's

not the objects themselves that are important, but the feelings and memories you associate with them. Look at your priorities in handling your income. Put off making any major purchases now.

- *Monday, September 12 (Moon into Aquarius, 4:29 pm)*
It's a number 3 day. Your attitude determines everything today. You communicate well. You're warm and receptive to what others say. Ease up on routines. Remain flexible. Enjoy the harmony, beauty and pleasures of life.

- *Tuesday, September 13 (Moon in Aquarius)*
The moon is in your third house today. You mental abilities are strong now and you have an emotional need to reinvigorate your studies, especially regarding matters of the past, Sadge. You're attracted to historical or archaeological studies. You write from as deep place today. It's a good day for journaling. Female relatives play a role in your day.

- *Wednesday, September 14 (Moon into Pisces, 9:23 pm)*
It's a number 5 day. You're versatile and changeable today. Think outside the box. Take risks, experiment. Approach the day with an unconventional mindset. Get a new point of view.

- *Thursday, September 15 (Moon in Pisces)*
The moon is in your fourth house today. It's a good day to stay close to home and take care of domestic matters. Work on a home repair project. Spend time with your family and loved ones. Get out and enjoy the summer and take time to smell the proverbial roses.

- *Friday, September 16 (Moon into Aries, 11:23 pm)*
There's a lunar eclipse in your fourth house today. You gain insight into a matter dealing with your home and domestic life. If you feel that you need to take control of matters, make sure that family members are aware of what you're doing. Whatever the issue that comes up, it's a serious one.

- *Saturday, September 17 (Moon in Aries)*
  The moon is in your fifth house today. It's a great day for pursuing a romance. There's more emotional depth in whatever you're doing now. You're creative and have the ability to tap deeply into the collective unconscious for inspiration. Children and pets could play a role.

- *Sunday, September 18 (Moon into Taurus, 11:59 pm)*
  It's a number 9 day. Finish what you started. Visualize the future; set your goals, then make them so. Look beyond the immediate. Get ready for something new. Strive for universal appeal.

- *Monday, September 19 (Moon in Taurus)*
  The moon is in your sixth house today. It's another service day. Others rely on you for help. So what else is new! Offer assistance, but don't deny your own needs. Visit someone who is ill, do a good deed. But pay attention to any health matters now. Exercise and watch your diet.

- *Tuesday, September 20 (Moon in Taurus)*
  It's a good time for gardening, cultivating ideas, doing practical things. While you maintain a common sense, down-to-earth perspective on life, you also long for the good life with its material blessings. Health and physical activity are highlighted.

- *Wednesday, September 21 (Moon into Gemini, 00:54 am)*
  It's number 3 day. Your attitude determines everything today. You communicate well. You're warm and receptive to what others say. Ease up on routines. Remain flexible. Enjoy the harmony, beauty and pleasures of life.

- *Thursday, September 22 (Moon in Gemini)*
  Mercury goes direct in your tenth house. Finally, thoughts about your career make more sense. Things aren't as dysfunctional as they seemed. You can deal with matters related to fellow workers. The last three weeks, which were probably frustrating and even nightmarish at times, should be seen as a learning experience, a time of growth for your

professional life. But you can only appreciate it now that it's over.

- *Friday, September 23 (Moon into Cancer, 3:34 am)*
Venus moves into your twelfth house today where it stays until October 18. There's nothing better now than solitude. Secrecy plays a role. You crave time alone to think things over, especially related to a romance. You might be wondering if someone special in your life now was also a friend in a past life.

- *Saturday, September 24 (Moon in Cancer)*
The moon is in your eighth house today. Take care of any matters related to taxes, insurance or investments. Be aware that emotions can get intense now, especially when dealing with shared resources. You could take an interest in a metaphysical topic now, such as life after death or past lives.

- *Sunday, September 25 (Moon into Leo, 8:49 am)*
It's a number 7 day. You're launching a journey into the unknown. Knowledge is essential to success. You're a spy for your own cause today. Go with the flow. Maintain your emotional balance, and don't make any absolute decisions until tomorrow.

- *Monday, September 26 (Moon in Leo)*
Pluto goes direct in your second house today, where it will remain until 2023. That releases more energy for dealing with money matters. You're moving forward and outward related to finances. Shared resources play a role. Keep in mind that Pluto transforms everything that is not needed.

- *Tuesday, September 27 (Moon into Virgo, 4:44 pm)*
Mars moves into your second house today. You're physically vital and it's a good time for handling money matters. There's strong energy in your fiscal house. You have an aggressive drive for security. There's also a tendency now to get into arguments over finances.

- *Wednesday, September 28 (Moon in Virgo)*
  The moon is in your tenth house today. Professional concerns
  are the focus of the day. Business dealings are highlighted. An
  advancement, a raise, or bonus is coming your way. Go for it,
  Sadge. You gain a boost of prestige.

- *Thursday, September 29 (Moon in Virgo)*
  Take care of details now, especially related to your health. Start
  exercising, watch your diet. Stop worrying and fretting. Take
  time to write in a journal. You write from a deep place now with
  lots of details and colorful descriptions.

- *Friday, September 30 (Moon into Libra, 2:54 am)*
  It's another number 3 day. Have fun today in preparation for
  tomorrow's discipline and focus. Make time to listen to others.
  Your charm and wit are appreciated. Spread your good news.
  You communicate well.

OCTOBER

- **Saturday, October 1 (Moon in Libra)**
  The moon is in your eleventh house today. You have deeper contact with friends now. You find strength in numbers and meaning through friends and groups, especially if you're working for the common good. Leo and Aries play a role in your day.

- **Sunday, October 2 (Moon into Scorpio, 2:44 pm)**
  It's a number 3 day. Take time to relax, enjoy yourself, recharge your batteries. You can influence people now with your upbeat attitude. Your charm and wit are appreciated. Foster generosity. In romance, you're an ardent lover and loyal.

- **Monday, October 3 (Moon in Scorpio)**
  The moon is in your twelfth house today. It's a great day for a mystical or spiritual discipline. Your intuition is heightened. Unconscious attitudes can be difficult now. So can relations with women. Keep your feelings secret. Follow your intuition.

- **Tuesday, October 4 (Moon in Scorpio)**
  You launch a journey into the unknown now. You become aware of confidential information, secret meetings, things happening behind closed doors. You investigate like a detective solving a mystery. Dig deep, gather information, but don't act on what you learn until tomorrow.

- **Wednesday, October 5 (Moon into Sagittarius, 3:27 am)**
  It's a number 6 day. Service to others is the theme of the day, and diplomacy wins the way. Do a good deed for someone. Visit

someone who is ill or someone in need of help. Focus on making people happy. A domestic adjustment works out for the best.

- *Thursday, October 6 (Moon in Sagittarius)*
  The moon is in your first house today. It's all about your health and your emotional self: how you feel and how you feel about yourself. Your feelings and thoughts are aligned. You get recharged for the rest of the month.

- *Friday, October 7 (Moon into Capricorn, 3:40 pm)*
  Mercury moves into your eleventh house today. That means that over the next three weeks you're communication skills will be strong, especially when dealing with a group in which you and others are working together with similar goals. Your friends provide you with a diversity of views.

- *Saturday, October 8 (Moon in Capricorn)*
  Your ambition and drive to succeed are highlighted. Your responsibilities increase. You may feel stressed and overworked, but don't ignore your exercise routine. Authority figures or elderly people play a role.

- *Sunday, October 9 (Moon in Capricorn)*
  The moon is in your second house today. You identify emotionally with your possessions or whatever you value. It's not the objects themselves that are important, but the feelings and memories you associate with them. Look at your priorities in handling your income. Put off making any major purchases now.

- *Monday, October 10 Moon into Aquarius, 1:33 am)*
  It's a number 2 day, putting the spotlight on cooperation. Help comes through friends, loved ones, especially a partner. Don't make waves. Don't rush or show resentment. Let things develop. There could be some soul-searching related to a relationship now.

- *Tuesday, October 11 (Moon in Aquarius)*
  The moon is in your third house today. Expect a lot of running around today, short trips here and there. After all, you're dealing with the everyday world. Try to group things together to cut down on your trips. You could have contact with neighbors or siblings today. Be careful talking on your cell and driving.

- *Wednesday, October 12 (Moon into Pisces, 7:43 am)*
  It's a number 4 day. Be practical with your money. Persevere to get things done today, and don't get sloppy. Control your impulses. Take care of your obligations. You're building foundations for an outlet for your creativity.

- *Thursday, October 13 (Moon in Pisces)*
  The moon is in your fourth house today. It's a good day to stay close to home and take care of domestic matters. Work on a home repair project. Spend time with your family and loved ones. Get out and enjoy the summer and take time to smell the proverbial roses.

- *Friday, October 14 (Moon into Aries, 10:09 am)*
  It's a number 6 day. Service to others is the theme of the day. You offer advice and support. Be diplomatic to anyone complaining or criticizing now. Try to make people happy. Be sympathetic, kind, and compassionate. But avoid scattering your energies.

- *Saturday, October 15 (Moon in Aries)*
  There's a full moon in your fifth house today. You reap what you've sown now related to a creative project. It's a good day to take a chance, experiment. In love, there's greater emotional depth to a relationship now. Alternately, you gain a better understanding of a child or children in your life.

- *Sunday, October 16 (Moon into Taurus, 10:05 am)*
  It's a number 8 day and it's your power day. So focus on a power play. You can go far with your plans and achieve financial success. Open your mind to a new approach that could bring in big bucks. It's a good day to buy a lotto ticket.

- *Monday, October 17 (Moon in Taurus)*
  The moon is in your sixth house today. It's a service day and you're at your best helping others now. You're the one others go to for guidance. Make yourself available, but don't deny your own needs. Keep your resolutions about exercise and watch your diet.

- *Tuesday, October 18 (Moon into Gemini, 9:31 am)*
  Venus moves into your first house today. Your self-awareness, your appearance is important now. You're dealing with the self and you feel great affection for the person you are becoming. You're physically vital, and relations with the opposite sex go very well now. You're also more appealing to the public.

- *Wednesday, October 19 (Moon in Gemini)*
  The moon is in your seventh house today. Marriage and partnerships take on new importance. There's harmony in a relationship. You might be socializing with associates from the workplace today and you get along well. You can fit in anywhere now.

- *Thursday, October 20 (Moon into Cancer, 10:29 am)*
  It's a number 3 day. Your attitude determines everything today. Spread your good news. You're innovative, creative and communicate well. Enjoy the harmony, beauty and pleasures of life. Beautify your home now, Sadge.

- *Friday, October 21 (Moon in Cancer)*
  The moon is in your eighth house now. Expect intense emotional experiences now. You have a strong sense of duty and feel obligated to fulfill your promises. Security is an important issue with you right now. You could be dealing your feelings about belongings and resources you possess, as well as things that you share with others.

- *Saturday, October 22 (Moon into Leo, 2:35 pm)*
  It's a number 5 day. Approach the day with an unconventional mindset. Release old structures, get a new point of view. Variety is the spice of life. You're versatile and changeable now, but don't spread yourself too thin.

- *Sunday, October 23 (Moon in Leo)*
  The moon is in your ninth house today. You're a dreamer and a thinker. You're captivated by new ideas and philosophies. You may feel a need to get away now, a break from the usual routine. You're feeling restless and yearn for something new.

- *Monday, October 24 (Moon into Virgo, 10:17 pm)*
  Mercury moves into your twelfth house today. Your decisions tend to be based on emotions rather than logic now. You tend to be secretive about your thoughts. You might be lacking confidence in a matter now, but you're also hiding it quite well.

- *Tuesday, October 25 (Moon in Virgo)*
  The moon is in your tenth house today. You're more responsive to the needs and moods of a group and of the public in general. You're open and accessible now, but take care to avoid emotional displays, especially in public. Your thoughts are focused on getting a raise, a promotion or a commendation for what you've done.

- *Wednesday, October 26 (Moon in Virgo)*
  Stick close to home, if possible. Focus on tidying up the house, attend to the detail and loose ends. You may exhibit some perfectionist tendencies now. Relax. Take time to write in a journal. You write from a deep place now with lots of details and colorful descriptions.

- *Thursday, October 27 (Moon into Libra, 8:52 am)*
  It's a number 1 day. That means you're at the top of your cycle, Sadge. You get a fresh start now. Be independent and avoid negative people. It's a great time for starting something new. Surround yourself with creative and adventurous people. Trust your hunches and don't be afraid to turn in a new direction.

- *Friday, October 28 (Moon in Libra)*
  The moon is in your eleventh house today. Friends play a key role in helping you fulfill your wishes and dreams. You get along well with groups, especially when everyone is of like-mind. You help the group's goals and you benefit in return.

- *Saturday, October 29 (Moon into Scorpio, 9:01 pm)*
  It's a number 3 day. Take time to relax, enjoy yourself, recharge your batteries for the month ahead. You can influence people now with your upbeat attitude. Your charm and wit are appreciated. Foster generosity. In romance, you're an ardent lover and loyal.

- *Sunday, October 30 (Moon in Scorpio)*
  There's a new moon in your twelfth house today. That means new personal opportunities arise related to whatever you're doing behind the scenes. Also look for new opportunities related to institutions, such as hospitals, courts, government offices. Something or someone from the past plays an important role.

- *Monday, October 31 (Moon in Scorpio)*
  Secrets, intrigue, confidential information play a role. You work best on your own today. Knowledge is essential to success. Gather information, but don't make any absolute decisions until tomorrow. Go with the flow.

NOVEMBER

- *Tuesday, November 1 (Moon into Sagittarius, 9:43 am)*
  It's a number 3 day. Take time to relax, enjoy yourself, and recharge your batteries. Have fun today in preparation for tomorrow's discipline and focus. Remain flexible in your schedule today. Foster generosity.

- *Wednesday, November 2 (Moon in Sagittarius)*
  The moon is in your first house today. It's all about your health and your emotional self: how you feel and how you feel about yourself. You may feel moody one moment, happy the next, then withdrawn and sad. It's difficult to remain detached and objective now. You're malleable and easily change your mind now.

- *Thursday, November 3 (Moon into Capricorn, 10:05 pm)*
  It's a number 6 day. Service to others is the theme of the day. You offer advice and support. Be sympathetic and kind, generous and tolerant. Focus on making people happy. Diplomacy wins the way.

- *Friday, November 4 (Moon in Capricorn)*
  The moon is in your second house today. Money and material goods are important to you now and give you a sense of security. You identify emotionally with your possessions or whatever you value. Watch your spending. You have a tendency to collect things and those objects make you feel at home and at peace.

- *Saturday, November 5 (Moon in Capricorn)*
  Your ambition and drive to succeed are highlighted. However, be aware that your responsibilities will increase. If you start to feel stressed and overworked, take time to shift gears and don't ignore your exercise routine. Authority figures or elderly people play a role.

- *Sunday, November 6 (Moon into Aquarius 8:56 am)*
  It's a number 9 day, Sadge. Complete a project now. Clear up odds and ends. Take an inventory on where things are going in your life. Make room for something new, but don't start anything today.

- *Monday, November 7 (Moon in Aquarius)*
  The moon is in your third house today. Take what you know and share it with others, Sadge. Look forward to a visit from relatives or siblings is likely, but keep conscious control of your emotions. Your thinking is unduly influenced by things of the past.

- *Tuesday, November 8 (Moon into Pisces, 4:46 pm)*
  It's a number 2 day and issues related to a relationship or partnership comes to a head. The spotlight is on cooperation now, but expect some soul-searching related to a relationship. New relationships are forming and help comes through friends.

- *Wednesday, November 9 (Moon in Pisces)*
  Mars moves into your third house and stays there until December 19. You're alert to subtle changes around you. You're quick thinking, resourceful, and ready to act. But try to avoid jumping to conclusions prematurely. You're very aggressive now and should take care to avoid arguments, especially with siblings and neighbors.

- *Thursday, November 10 (Moon into Aries, 8:46 pm)*
  It's a number 4 day, and a good one to spend time on getting organized. Take care of your obligations and control your impulses to wander off. Persevere to get things done. You're building a foundation for the future. Hard work is called for now.

- *Friday, November 11 (Moon in Aries)*
  Venus moves into Capricorn, your second house today. That means financial matters go well. You equate your financial assets with emotional security now. You have a tendency to collect things and those objects make you feel at home and at peace. It's not the objects themselves that are important, but the feelings and memories you associate with them.

- *Saturday, November 12 (Moon into Taurus, 9:25 pm)*
  Mercury moves into your first house today. You're very expressive and happy to talk about your ideas and about yourself now. You have the ability to make connections between differing subjects that others overlook. You can also adapt quickly to changing circumstances, and easily pick up new and useful information.

- *Sunday, November 13 (Moon in Taurus)*
  With the moon in your sixth house today, the emphasis turns to your daily work and health. Service to others is the theme of the day, Sadge. Look for ways to move ahead. You're in the driver's seat now. Be careful not to overlook any seemingly minor matters that could take on importance. Keep up with your exercise plan and watch your diet.

- *Monday, November 14 (Moon into Gemini, 8:24 pm)*
  With the full moon in your sixth house today, yesterday's energy flows into your Monday. It's also a time of completion, especially related to service to others. You reap what you've sown. You also gain insight into a health matter.

- *Tuesday, November 15 (Moon in Gemini)*
  The moon is in your seventh house today. Marriage and partnerships take on new importance. There's harmony in a relationship. You might be socializing with associates from the workplace today and you get along well. You can fit in anywhere now.

- *Wednesday, November 16 (Moon into Cancer, 7:58 pm)*
  It's a number 1 day. That means you're at the top of your cycle again. You get a fresh start now. Be independent and avoid negative people. It's a great time for starting something new. Surround yourself with creative and adventurous people. Trust your hunches and don't be afraid to turn in a new direction.

- *Thursday November 17 (Moon in Cancer)*
  The moon is in your eighth house today. Things tend to get more emotionally intense than usual, especially if you're dealing with shared resources or belongings. You could attract the attention of powerful people now. It's a good day to look into any issues related to taxes, insurance, or investments.

- *Friday, November 18 (Moon into Leo, 10:15 pm)*
  It's a number 3 day. Take time to relax, enjoy yourself, recharge your batteries. You can influence people now with your upbeat attitude. Your charm and wit are appreciated. Foster generosity. In romance, you're an ardent lover and loyal.

- *Saturday, November 19 (Moon in Leo)*
  Neptune goes direct in your fourth house today. Your inspiration is soaring. You can tap into higher energy. Your spirituality is heightened. Any trouble with children could result in confusion due to lack of information. You find it helpful to spend time in meditation, the deeper the better.

- *Sunday, November 20 (Moon in Leo)*
  The moon is in your ninth house today. You can create positive change through your ideas. You guide others in their intellectual development, especially related philosophy, mythology or religion. A foreign born person or a foreign country plays a role in your day.

- *Saturday, November 21 (Moon into Virgo, 4:35 am)*
  It's a number 6 day. Be understanding and avoid confrontations. Diplomacy wins the way. Focus on making people happy, but avoid scattering your energies. Be sympathetic, kind, and compassionate.

- *Sunday, November 22 (Moon in Virgo)*
  The moon is in your tenth house today. Your life is more public today. You're more responsive to the needs and moods of a group and of the public in general. Avoid any emotional displays in public, such as at a company gathering.

- *Wednesday, November 23 (Moon into Libra, 2:43 pm)*
  It's a number 8 day, your power day, your day to play it your way. Expect a financial windfall. It's a good day to play the lotto. Business dealings go well. A new approach could bring in big bucks.

- *Thursday, November 24 (Moon in Libra)*
  With the moon in your eleventh house today, friends play an important role, especially Aries and Leo. Take a look at your goals today and make sure that they're still an expression of who you are. You do well in a group setting. You could be dealing with an issue involving social consciousness. Happy Thanksgiving.

- *Friday, November 25 (Moon in Libra)*
  Romance is highlighted. Relationships issues figure prominently. It's a day for feeding your creative juices. Plan an adventurous encounter with a friend. Your personal grace, magnetism and physical attraction play a role.

- *Saturday, November 26 (Moon into Scorpio, 3:02 am)*
  It's a number 2 day, and that means you continue to explore the theme of partnership. Your spouse or partner is at your side. Don't make waves or show resentment, but take time again today to consider the direction you're headed and your motivation for continuing on this path. Your intuition focuses on relationships.

- *Sunday, November 27 (Moon in Scorpio)*
  The moon is in your twelfth house today. Think carefully before you act today. Hide your moodiness. There's a tendency now to undo all the positive actions you've taken. Avoid any self-destructive tendencies. Be aware of hidden enemies.

- *Monday, November 28 (Moon into Sagittarius, 3:46 pm)*
  It's a number 4 day. Your organizational skills are highlighted. Control your impulses. Set aside romantic notions for the time being. Persevere and fulfill your obligations. You're building foundations for your creativity. Emphasize quality.

- *Tuesday, November 29 (Moon in Sagittarius)*
  There's a new moon in your first house today. It's all about new opportunities with lots of energy flowing your way in the coming month. Get ready. Changes are coming your way. You're restless and feeling a surge of independence. You've got lots of ideas, and need to stay focused.

- *Wednesday, November 30 (Moon in Sagittarius)*
  The moon is on your ascendant. The way you see yourself now is the way others see you. You're recharged for the month ahead and this makes you more appealing to the public. You're physically vital, and relations with the opposite sex go well.

DECEMBER

- *Thursday, December 1 (Moon into Capricorn, 3:53 am)*
It's a number 4 day. Your organizational skills are highlighted. Control your impulses. Hard work is called for now. Tear down the old in order to rebuild. Be methodical and thorough. Emphasize quality. It's not a good day for romance.

- *Friday, December 2 (Moon in Capricorn)*
The moon is in your second house today. You studiously looks for new ways of making money, analyzing the possibilities. At the same time, you identify emotionally with your possessions or whatever you value. In that sense, money and material goods gives you a sense of security. You also see money-making schemes as a path to freedom and flexibility.

- *Saturday, December 3 (Moon into Aquarius, 2:45 pm)*
It's a number 6 day. Service to others is the theme of the day. Focus on making people happy. You offer advice and support. Be sympathetic and kind, generous and tolerant. However, avoid scattering your energies.

- *Sunday, December 4 (Moon in Aquarius)*
The moon is in your third house today. That means your mental abilities are strong and you have an emotional need to reinvigorate your studies. You also could be exploring matters from the deep past. Take what you know and share it with others. It's a good time to pursue a challenging mental activity, such as on-line gaming, a debate, or a game of chess, anything that challenges your mental prowess.

- *Monday December 5 (Moon into Pisces, 11:32 pm)*
  It's a number 8 day, your power day, Sadge. You're in the power seat, so focus on a power play. You have a chance to expand, to gain recognition, fame, even power. It's a good day to buy a lotto ticket. Expect a windfall.

- *Tuesday, December 6 (Moon in Pisces)*
  The moon is in your fourth house today. You're feeling close to your roots. You're dealing with the foundations of the person you're becoming. It's a good day to spend time on a home improvement project. Stick close to home, if possible. Friends play a role in your day.

- *Wednesday, December 7 (Moon in Pisces)*
  Venus moves into your third house today. Your positive relationship with siblings and relatives works to your benefit. You mental abilities are strong now and you have an emotional need to reinvigorate your studies, especially regarding matters of the past. It's a good time for writing and getting your work published.

- *Thursday December 8 (Moon into Aries, 5:17 am)*
  It's a number 2 day. Cooperation and partnerships are highlighted today. Show your appreciation to others. Use your intuition to get a sense of your day. There could be some soul searching related to relationships.

- *Friday, December 9 (Moon in Aries)*
  The moon is in your fifth house today. Your love life takes off now. There's an idealistic turn to whatever you do for pleasure. It's a great time for a creative project, especially fiction writing. You could be somewhat possessive of loved ones and children today. It's also a good day to get a pet!

- *Saturday, December 10 (Moon into Taurus, 7:42 am)*
  It's a number 4 day. Persevere to get things done today. Tear down the old in order to rebuild. You're building a creative base for your future. Be methodical and thorough. Missing papers or objects are found.

- *Sunday, December 11 (Moon in Taurus)*
  With the moon in your sixth house today, the emphasis turns to your daily work and service to others. Let go of the big picture for now, Sadge, and attend to all the details. Be careful not to overlook any seemingly minor matters that could take on importance. Keep up with your exercise plan and watch your diet.

- *Monday, December 12 (Moon into Gemini, 7:42 am)*
  It's a number 6 day. Yesterday's energy flows into your Monday. Service to others is the theme of the day. Focus on making people happy. You offer advice and support. Be diplomatic rather than confrontational. Do a good deed for someone. Visit someone who is ill or someone in need of help.

- *Tuesday, December 13 (Moon in Gemini)*
  There's a full moon in your seventh house today. It's a time of completion. You reap what you've sown, especially related to partnerships. Focus on relationships now. You can gain new insight into friendships now.

- *Wednesday, December 14 (Moon into Cancer, 7:09 am)*
  It's another number 8 day, your power day, your day to play it your way. Expect a financial windfall. It's a good day to play the lotto. Business dealings go well. A new approach brings in big bucks.

- *Thursday December 15 (Moon in Cancer)*
  The moon is in your eighth house now. Expect intense emotional experiences now. You have a strong sense of duty and feel obligated to fulfill your promises. Security is an important issue with you right now. You could be dealing your feelings about belongings and things you possess, as well as things that you share with others, such as a spouse.

- *Friday, December 16 (Moon into Leo, 8:15 am)*
  It's a number 1 day. That means you're at the top of your cycle again. You get a fresh start now. Be independent and avoid

negative people. It's a great time for starting something new. Surround yourself with creative and adventurous people, Sadge. Trust your hunches and don't be afraid to turn in a new direction.

- *Saturday, December 17 (Moon in Leo)*
  The moon is in your ninth house today. You're a dreamer and a thinker. You're very receptive to new ideas and your imagination runs wild now. You're an explorer, Sadge, searching for a higher truth, and you want to inform and guide others with what you've learned.

- *Sunday, December 18 (Moon into Virgo, 12:52 pm)*
  It's a number 3 day for you. You're innovative, creative and communicate well now. You can be blunt, but for now you're getting along well with others. You're warm and receptive to what others say. Enjoy the harmony, beauty and pleasures of life. Intuition is highlighted.

- *Monday, December 19 (Moon in Virgo)*
  Mars moves into your fourth house today, bolstering your urge to initiate new things. You have an aggressive drive to attain security now. You're very protective of the home front. You're probably busy fixing things around your house, maybe even installing a home security system. Be aware that you could become overly abrupt with others, especially family members. Back off in order to avoid disagreements.

- *Tuesday, December 20 (Moon into Libra, 9:40 pm)*
  It's a number 5 day. That means it's a good day to promote new ideas. You're versatile, changeable. Be careful not to spread out and diversify too much. Freedom of thought and action are key. A change of scenery would work to your advantage

- *Wednesday, December 21 (Moon in Libra)*
  The moon is in your eleventh house today. Friends play a key role in helping you fulfill your wishes and dreams. You get along well with groups, especially when everyone is of like-mind. You

help the group's goals and you benefit in return. Friends play a key role in helping you fulfill your wishes and dreams.

- *Thursday, December 22 (Moon in Libra)*
  Romance is highlighted today, Sadge. Your creativity, personal grace and magnetism are emphasized. It's a great day to schedule an adventurous encounter with your significant other. Museums, art, music all figure in your day.

- *Friday, December 23 (Moon into Scorpio, 9:33 am)*
  It's a number 8 day, another power day, and you're in the power seat today, Sadge. You pull a financial coup. Business dealings go well. Open your mind to a new approach that could bring in big bucks.

- *Saturday, December 24 (Moon in Scorpio)*
  The moon is in your twelfth house today. It's a great day for a mystical or spiritual discipline. Your intuition is heightened. Unconscious attitudes can be difficult now. So can relations with women. Keep your feelings secret. Follow your intuition.

- *Sunday, December 25 (Moon into Sagittarius, 10:20 pm)*
  It's a number 1 day. That means you're at the top of your cycle again. You get a fresh start now. Be independent and bold, and avoid negative people. It's a great time for starting something new. Surround yourself with creative and adventurous people. Trust your hunches and don't be afraid to turn in a new direction. Merry Christmas!

- *Monday, December 26 (Moon in Sagittarius)*
  The moon is on your ascendant. Your appearance and personality shine. You feelings and thoughts are aligned today. You're physically vital, and relations with the opposite sex go well. You're recharged and this makes you more appealing to the public.

- *Tuesday, December 27 (Moon in Sagittarius)*
  The moon is in your first house today. It's all about the emotional self now, Sadge. You have strong feelings related to your appearance,

your self-awareness, the person you are becoming. You also could be feeling strongly about a personal health issue, or about details that you've overlooked regarding a matter of importance. You're ready to move ahead.

- *Wednesday, December 28 (Moon into Capricorn, 10:13 am)*
There's a new moon in your second house today. That means you can expect new opportunities for making money. You gain a greater sense of security now. You feel best at home surrounded by your favorite possessions. It's not the objects themselves that are important, but the feelings and memories you associate with them.

- *Thursday, December 29 (Moon in Capricorn)*
With Uranus going direct in your fifth house today, you feel a strong need to focus on a creative project. You want to do it your own way now, and as a result, you might isolate yourself. You tend to act impulsively now and you could be in for some surprises. Children could play a role.

- *Friday, December 30 (Moon into Aquarius 8:30 pm)*
It's a number 6 day. Diplomacy wins the way. Service to others is the theme of the day. You offer advice and support. Focus on making people happy. Be sympathetic, kind, and compassionate.

- *Saturday, December 31 (Moon in Aquarius)*
The moon is in your third house. You're busy keeping your mind occupied with new information. You study the details, especially those that relate to the past. Take what you know and share it with others. Siblings and relatives play a role. Happy New Year!

ABOUT THE AUTHORS

For ten years, Trish and Rob MacGregor wrote the Sydney Omarr's Day-by-Day Astrological Guides. Trish is also the author of *Unlocking the Secrets of Scorpio* (2015), and nine other astrology books. In addition, the MacGregors are the authors of *The Synchronicity Highway, Aliens in the Backyard, The 7 Secrets of Synchronicity* and *Synchronicity & the Other Side*. Both are also novelists and have each won the Edgar Allan Poe Award from the Mystery Writers of America. Trish's most recent novel is *Apparition* and Rob's latest novel is *Time Catcher*. They can be contacted at: blog.synchrosecrets.com

Curious about other Crossroad Press books?
Stop by our site:
http://store.crossroadpress.com
We offer quality writing
in digital, audio, and print formats.

Enter the code FIRSTBOOK
to get 20% off your first order from our store!
Stop by today!

CPSIA information can be obtained at www.ICGtesting.com
Printed in the USA
BVOW06s2021170216

437034BV00003B/31/P